The Case for People's Quantitative Easing

Frances Coppola

The Case for People's Quantitative Easing

polity

First published in 2019 by Polity Press
Reprinted: 2019 (four times)

Polity Press
65 Bridge Street
Cambridge CB2 1UR, UK

Polity Press
101 Station Landing
Suite 300
Medford, MA 02155, USA

ISBN-13: 978-1-5095-3129-5 (hardback)
ISBN-13: 978-1-5095-3130-1 (paperback)

A catalogue record for this book is available from the British Library.

Library of Congress Cataloging-in-Publication Data
Names: Coppola, Frances, author.
Title: The case for people's quantitative easing / Frances Coppola.
Description: Medford, MA : Polity, 2019. | Series: The case for |
Identifiers: LCCN 2018059985 (print) | LCCN 2019009044 (ebook) |
    ISBN 9781509531325 (Epub) | ISBN 9781509531295 (hardback) |
    ISBN 9781509531301 (paperback)
Subjects: LCSH: Quantitative easing (Monetary policy) | Economic policy. | BISAC:
    POLITICAL SCIENCE / Public Policy / Economic Policy.
Classification: LCC HG230.3 (ebook) | LCC HG230.3 .C67 2019 (print) | DDC
    339.5/3--dc23
LC record available at https://lccn.loc.gov/2018059985

Typeset in 11 on 15 Sabon by Servis Filmsetting Ltd, Stockport, Cheshire
Printed and bound in the United States by LSC Communications

For further information on Polity, visit our website: politybooks.com

Contents

Introduction

After the financial crisis of 2008, a new phrase entered the lexicon – 'Quantitative Easing', or QE. As people lost their jobs, defaulted on debts and lost their homes, and banks and businesses failed, central banks feared a repeat of the Depression of the 1930s. To ward it off, they poured money into the economy. They did so by buying assets – their own government's debt, government-guaranteed assets such as mortgage-backed securities issued by quasi-government agencies, and in some cases corporate stocks and bonds. They paid for the assets with newly created money, which went directly into deposit accounts in commercial banks. As a result, money 'in circulation' ballooned, while interest rates fell to historic lows.

But the money didn't circulate to the places where it was really needed. The problem with asset

Introduction

purchases is that assets are owned mainly by the rich, and the rich don't need to spend money. So, when they sold their assets, they simply reinvested the money in other assets. Prices of prime real estate in city centres soared. Oil prices, commodity prices and the prices of essential foodstuffs soared. Stock prices rose to extraordinary heights. Corporate bond yields fell to unprecedented lows.

In theory, rising stock prices and falling corporate bond yields should have encouraged corporations to invest. But they didn't. Instead, corporations borrowed cheaply to buy back their stocks. This flattered their return on equity, but it didn't create jobs.

Meanwhile, the expensively bailed-out banks were not lending. Pressured by regulators, their focus was on repairing their balance sheets and making themselves safer. So they cut back riskier lending such as loans to small businesses, and they made it more difficult for ordinary people to obtain mortgages and borrow for consumer spending. QE increased their reserves, but it didn't encourage them to lend. And people didn't want to borrow, either. Many had lost their jobs, or suffered falls in their real income due to stagnant wages, benefit cutbacks and inflation. Many were already highly indebted and unable or unwilling to take on more

2

debt. So not only were banks not lending, people weren't borrowing. People began to ask why banks could be bailed out, but not people. If repairing the economy means getting people to spend more, wouldn't it be better to give money directly to people?

This book argues that giving money directly to people is the best way of restoring damaged economies. When the next crisis comes – and come it will – 'QE for the People' should be the policy tool of choice.

1

The Great Experiment

'They did not have to be so unfair'

On 15 September 2008 the biggest financial shock for decades struck Wall Street, as the investment bank Lehman Brothers filed for bankruptcy. Even though Lehman had been teetering on the brink of insolvency for the previous week, and there had been emergency talks with potential rescuers, no one expected it to fail. Surely, if no rescuer could be found, it would be bailed out, just as the mortgage giants Fannie Mae and Freddie Mac had been only two weeks before?

But the US Treasury saw no reason to bail it out. Lehman Brothers was an unregulated investment bank. It did not deal with the savings of ordinary Americans. Nor did it lend to ordinary American businesses or households. Allowing it to fail would send a message to other unregulated banks that they should get their houses in order.

The day after Lehman's failure, the Federal Reserve took over the American insurance giant AIG. AIG had sold credit default swaps to all of the world's major banks, and now they were claiming on their insurance. It was bleeding to death – but if it failed, it would take all those banks down with it. The Fed's bailout prevented a global financial system meltdown, though buying AIG cost the Fed $85 billion. The decision to allow Lehman to fail was already looking expensive. But there was much worse to come.

As the impact of Lehman's collapse rippled out through the financial system, asset prices crashed and banks started to fail. Ben Bernanke, Chairman of the Federal Reserve, and Hank Paulson, US Treasury Secretary, asked Congress for $700 billion to buy toxic assets from troubled banks. The Bill authorizing it was passed on 3 October. The bailout became known as the 'Troubled Assets Relief Program' (TARP).[1] It was the first – but by no means the last – asset-purchase programme in the aftermath of Lehman's failure.

Despite its name, TARP made few asset purchases. Pricing toxic assets was simply too difficult. So, instead, the US Treasury purchased preference shares in distressed banks. Half of the TARP money went into buying banks. Nor were banks the only things the Treasury bought with TARP money. The giant carmakers GM and Chrysler received injections of, respectively, \$51bn and \$12.5bn, with a further \$17.2bn going to GM's banking arm GMAC (Ally Financial).[2]

The one group that didn't benefit from TARP was homeowners. TARP was supposed to provide assistance to people at risk of losing their homes. But very little of the TARP money was used for that purpose. Banks, financial institutions and big corporations were all bailed out. But an estimated five million Americans lost their homes in the Great Recession. Why weren't homeowners bailed out?

A significant obstacle was the nature of the American mortgage market. Unlike British and European mortgages, American mortgages are generally not held on the books of banks. They are sold on to giant warehouses, which package them up into securities and sell them to investors in the capital markets. Prior to the financial crisis, these 'residential mortgage-backed securities' (RMBS) were rated as prime quality assets, with low stable returns and minimal default risk. Pension funds and insurance companies invested in billions of dollars' worth of them. The retirement savings of millions of Americans were thus invested in the mortgages of millions more Americans.

Since one person's debt is another person's asset, when you write off a debt, you also write off an asset. Writing off the mortgages underlying the securities would have wiped out the retirement savings of all those Americans. Debt jubilee for borrowers would have been Armageddon for savers and pensioners.

An alternative might have been to have paid off the mortgages, rather than writing them off. The cost would have been enormous – estimates were as high as \$750bn.[3] But the TARP programme provided \$700bn to banks and financial institutions, and there were other financial injections too. The total cost of bailing out financial institutions and corporations was far more than \$750bn. Why could the US afford to bail out financial institutions and corporations, but not ordinary people?

Underlying the US government's reluctance to assist homeowners was a belief that they deserved their fate.[4] People who lost their homes had borrowed recklessly, so should not be bailed out. This was to some degree true: property speculation was rife before the crash, and some borrowers were simply trying to profit from the bubble before it crashed.

But not everyone was a property speculator. Many of those who lost their homes had bought with a large mortgage at the top of the market. When the market crashed, and the economy followed, they ended up with a house worth less than the mortgage, and no job. So they handed in the keys and walked away. The problem was that separating out the 'deserving' homeowner from the 'undeserving' was just too complex. There was insufficient information about borrowers to be able to judge whether they were opportunists looking to make a quick return or families wanting a home. Some were both.

Whatever the reasons, the fact remains that few homeowners received help. *The Economist* magazine, in a piece entitled 'They did not have to be so unfair', highlighted the legacy of popular anger:

> The US government cared a lot more about saving the incumbent banks and bankers than it did about helping regular Americans blindsided by the collapse of the housing market and the ensuing contraction. As a result, many Americans now believe that the rules are rigged against them for the benefit of a few politically connected financial speculators: privatized gains and socialized losses. It is difficult to disagree.[5]

Over the next decade, central banks and governments around the world were to spend an extraordinary amount of money on bailing out banks and propping up financial markets. Meanwhile, ordinary people, deprived of money by austerity-minded governments, risk-averse banks and miserly corporations, were forced to tighten their belts. The decade from 2008 to 2018 could perhaps be dubbed the Great Unfairness. But it has another name too – the Great Experiment.

Lessons from the Great Depression

Pouring money into banks and financial markets prevented the financial system from melting down. But it did not protect people from the economic consequences of bankers' folly. As business failures and job losses mounted, the United States slid into the deepest recession since the 1930s. Fearing a repeat of the Great Depression of 1929–33 – the worst economic downturn of the twentieth century – the Federal Reserve cut interest rates to nearly zero and embarked on QE. As the Great Recession spread out across the world, other central banks followed suit, cutting interest rates to near-zero, supporting damaged banks, and doing various forms of QE. Governments joined in too, pouring money into their economies in a coordinated programme of fiscal stimulus.[6] The Great Experiment had begun.

Like the Great Recession, the Great Depression started with a financial crisis – the Wall Street Crash of 1929. And like the Great Recession, it rippled out across the world. The misery of the Great Depression has been documented by writers such as Steinbeck[7] and recorded in photographs from the time. The economic causes of the Great Depression have been extensively studied, and the policy responses to the Great Depression at the time have been seriously criticized.

One of the sternest critics of the Federal Reserve's response to the Great Depression was Milton Friedman. He is the father of QE and the ultimate architect of the Great Experiment. In his pioneering book with Anna Schwartz, Friedman documented the changes in the money supply during the Great Depression (or the Great Contraction, as he and Schwartz termed it).[8] As the Depression progressed, people stopped keeping money on deposit at the bank. Although the reduction in bank deposits was partially offset by rising holdings of physical currency, the total amount of money in circulation – bank deposits plus currency – fell by one third between 1929 and 1933.

Friedman concluded that it was the collapse in the money stock that turned a recession into a

Depression. And he said that this could have been prevented:

> Different, and feasible actions by the monetary authorities could have prevented the decline in the stock of money – indeed, could have produced almost any desired increase in the money stock . . .
>
> Prevention or moderation of the decline in the stock of money, let alone the substitution of monetary expansion, would have reduced the contraction's severity and almost as certainly its duration.[9]

Friedman proposed that in a disastrous economic slump such as the Great Depression, monetary authorities should put money directly into the economy. In 1968, in his book 'The Optimum Quantity of Money and other Essays', he suggested a novel way of doing it.[10] 'Let us suppose now that one day a helicopter flies over this community and drops an additional $1,000 in bills from the sky', he said. 'And let us suppose further that everyone is convinced that this is a unique event which will never be repeated.'[11]

Friedman's 'helicopter drop' is a powerful image. Imagine New York's famous 'ticker-tape' parade, but with real money instead of shredded paper. Banknotes fluttering down from the sky and littering the streets. People rushing to pick them up, perhaps fighting over them, maybe sharing them out. Groups of people might arrive with brooms, sweeping up the banknotes into piles so that they can be more easily collected. Street vendors would arrive, selling food and drink to those collecting the money. Shops in the area would stay open for longer, bring in additional stock, hire extra sales staff to go out into the streets and entice the money-collectors into the shops. Banks, too, might stay open so that people could deposit their windfalls for later use. Everyone would try to get a piece of the money, one way or another. It would resemble a feeding frenzy. And indeed, that is what it would be. We can't eat money, but we can buy food with it, and other things that we need or want. Additional money gives us more purchasing power, and that encourages businesses to produce more.

Friedman was not the only economist to observe that disturbances in the behaviour of money were a major cause of the Great Depression. Irving Fisher, writing at the height of the Great Depression, described how debt defaults and bank failures caused real interest rates to rise and prices to fall catastrophically in a devastating feedback loop:

Unless some counteracting cause comes along to prevent the fall in the price level, such a depression as that of 1929–1933 (namely when the more the debtors pay the more they owe) tends to continue, going deeper, in a vicious spiral, for many years. There is then no tendency of the boat to stop tipping until it has capsized. Ultimately, of course, but only after almost universal bankruptcy, the indebtedness must cease to grow greater and begin to grow less. Then comes recovery and a tendency for a new boom-depression sequence. This is the so-called 'natural' way out of a depression, via needless and cruel bankruptcy, unemployment, and starvation.[12]

The British economist John Maynard Keynes, also drawing on his experience of the Depression, pointed out that when people stop spending and hoard money like crazy, the economy goes into a slump. He described how, when interest rates are very low, the economy can become caught in a 'liquidity trap' in which investors prefer to hold cash rather than invest in riskier, but more productive, stocks and bonds:

... after the rate of interest has fallen to a certain level, liquidity preference may become virtually absolute in the sense that almost everyone prefers [holding] cash [rather than] holding a debt which yields so low a rate of interest ...[13]

Fisher's theory of 'debt deflation' and Keynes's 'liquidity trap' have all featured in economic critiques of the Great Experiment. But it is Friedman's 'helicopter drop' that lies at the heart of the Great Experiment.

Japan's long stagnation

Friedman thought that maintaining the stock of money would prevent the frightening deflationary collapse of the 1930s. But other economists argued that 'helicopter money' should also be used to prevent the mild deflation that is often associated with economic stagnation. The most influential of these was Ben Bernanke, the Chairman of the Federal Reserve at the time of the 2008 financial crisis – because he had the opportunity to put his theory into practice.

Mild deflation can be benign. Falling prices benefit consumers, because it enables them to purchase more goods and services. However, price falls should be short-lived, as either demand will rise or supply will fall (or both), thus stabilizing the price at some level. This is called 'market clearing', and in efficient markets it should occur rapidly. Sustained mild deflation is a sign that markets are not functioning normally. When prices continually fall, people tend to defer non-essential spending decisions in anticipation of lower prices. This discourages businesses from investing, hiring and paying good wages. The result can be economic stagnation.

After the collapse of its banks in 1990, Japan experienced a long period of economic stagnation. There was no deflationary collapse, but prices fell by about one per cent per year, despite the Bank of Japan cutting interest rates to zero. By 2000, people had come to expect continually falling prices. Consumer spending was low, business investment was on the floor and Japan's economy was stubbornly in recession. Deflation and stagnation seemed to be here to stay. Determined to resist this, the Bank of Japan tried a new approach. In March 2001, it began to purchase large quantities of financial assets, expanding its purchases in November that year. This was the first major experiment with what we now know as QE.

In a speech in 2002, Bernanke argued that deflation and stagnation persisted in Japan because of inadequate action by the Japanese government and the Bank of Japan.[14] If they were to act more aggressively, the slump would come to an end. But what should they do? Bernanke's prescription was similar to Friedman's. He gave the following example to explain how increasing the money supply will always raise inflation:

The US government has a technology, called a printing press (or, today, its electronic equivalent), that allows it to produce as many US dollars as it wishes at essentially no cost. By increasing the number of US dollars in circulation, or even by credibly threatening to do so, the US government can also reduce the value of a dollar in terms of goods and services, which is equivalent to raising the prices in dollars of those goods and services. We conclude that, *under a paper-money system, a determined government can always generate higher spending and hence positive inflation.*

[my emphasis]

He went on to list a variety of methods that governments could use to raise inflation. Among them is this:

A broad-based tax cut, for example, accommodated by a programme of open-market purchases to alleviate any tendency for interest rates to increase, would almost certainly be an effective stimulant to consumption and hence to prices. Even if households decided not to increase consumption but instead re-balanced their portfolios by using their extra cash to acquire real and financial assets, the resulting increase in asset values would lower the cost of capital and improve the balance sheet positions of potential borrowers. *A money-financed tax cut is essentially equivalent to Milton Friedman's famous 'helicopter drop' of money.*

[my emphasis]

After this comment, Bernanke became popularly known as 'Helicopter Ben'. Instead of Bernanke's money-financed tax cut, the Japanese central bank continued to buy large quantities of Japanese government bonds. It expected that this would increase credit creation and spur higher spending, which in turn should raise inflation. But five years later, with inflation still at zero, the Bank of Japan stopped its purchases.

Why did QE fail in Japan? The economist Richard Koo argued that it was the wrong medicine. Diagnosing Japan's problem as an overhang of bad debt on household and corporate balance sheets, he observed that when people are highly indebted, they pay down debt rather than taking on more. When large numbers of households and corporations are paying down debt simultaneously, this causes a form of economic stagnation that he termed a 'balance sheet recession'.[15] In a balance sheet recession, monetary policy is ineffective. Lowering interest rates and throwing money at banks cannot increase credit creation, since no one wants to borrow. Koo argued that a better response would be money distribution by the fiscal authority – namely, deficit spending. In this respect he, like Bernanke – and unlike the Japanese central bank – was true to the spirit of Friedman's original concept of a 'helicopter drop'.

Koo's views failed to gain mainstream attention. The consensus view among economists was that the Bank of Japan had not convinced anyone it was really committed to raising inflation. Bernanke said that the reason QE had failed to raise inflation was that the Bank of Japan hadn't done enough of it. Part of the purpose of the Great Experiment was to prove Bernanke right.

The failure of the Great Experiment

Friedman envisaged helicopter money as a short, sharp stimulus to shock a deflationary economy out of its slump. This was indeed how QE was used immediately after the 2008 crisis, and initially it seemed to work. The Great Recession was short lived. QE stabilized asset prices, very low interest rates prevented widespread debt defaults, and continual transfusions of central bank money into banks and financial markets prevented the payments system – the 'circulatory system' of the economy – from seizing up. The feared Depression did not materialize. By 2010, most economies were starting to recover.

But there was a price for this recovery. Government budget deficits expanded as financial and other corporations were bailed out, tax revenues fell, and unemployment benefits rose. As a result, government debt rapidly increased. In addition, the recession knocked a huge hole in 'gross domestic product' (GDP), a measure of national income. As government debt is usually quoted as a proportion of GDP, the combination of rising debt with falling GDP caused government debt burdens to rise rapidly.

In 2009, the economists Carmen Reinhart and Kenneth Rogoff published a research paper purporting to show that government debt/GDP ratio above ninety per cent spelled disaster.[16] Their calculations were eventually shown to be fatally flawed: although high debt is associated with slow growth there is no clear causal link, and there is no tipping point at ninety per cent or anywhere else. But this information did not come to light until some years later.[17] By that time, the damage had been done. Suddenly, countries that had previously been paragons of fiscal rectitude appeared to be on the verge of default. Others, more fragile before the crisis (though not necessarily worse managed), needed the help of the IMF. Advanced economies looked at least as risky as emerging markets.

Then Greece blew up. In early 2010, the highly indebted Aegean country admitted it could not pay its debts, and was forced to accept what would become the first of several bailouts. This was accompanied by harsh spending cuts and tax rises designed to restore confidence in its ability to honour its obligations. However, the austerity programme had exactly the opposite effect: Greece's economy slid into deep recession. In 2012, it restructured its private sector debt and accepted a second bailout from its fellow Eurozone countries in tandem with the IMF, again in return for draconian 'reforms' that, far from restoring it to health, significantly worsened its economic situation.

Right-wing politicians shamelessly exploited Greece's disaster and Reinhart and Rogoff's research to shift the popular focus away from repairing the economy towards reducing government indebtedness. Their tactics worked. Fearing Greece's fate, people accepted austerity. From 2010 onwards, governments stopped putting money into their economies and started to withdraw it by imposing spending cuts and tax rises. Far from generating robust recovery, spending cuts and tax rises squashed what little economic growth there was. As the recovery fizzled out, central banks tried to sustain it by doing more QE. Over the next eight years, central banks poured ever more money into their economies, while governments drained ever more out.

Some governments, such as the UK's coalition government, explicitly relied on central banks to dampen the economic effects of spending cuts and tax rises. In a speech at the Mansion House in April 2013, George Osborne, then the UK's Chancellor of the Exchequer, outlined his strategy for recovery:

> First, active monetary policy to support demand and help keep lending rates low. That is anchored by a tough, credible fiscal policy that bears down on our excessive deficit, the second element of our plan. Finally, far-reaching structural reform to improve the supply potential of our economy – the only lasting way to raise our nation's living standards and succeed in the global race.[18]

It is hard not to see this as an explicit instruction to the incoming Governor of the Bank of England, Mark Carney, who was present in the Mansion House when Osborne gave the speech. Although

Osborne appeared to suggest that monetary policy would be 'anchored' by fiscal consolidation, the boot was on the other foot. Osborne relied on low interest rates, QE and other Bank of England initiatives such as Funding for Lending to prevent fiscal austerity causing a double-dip recession.

Osborne was not the only finance minister who relied on the central bank to keep the show on the road. In 2012, the President of the European Central Bank, Mario Draghi, announced that the ECB would do 'whatever it takes' to prevent the euro imploding.[19] After this, governments across the Eurozone embarked on fiscal consolidation programmes, secure in the knowledge that the ECB had their back. In some cases, the ECB helped to enforce fiscal austerity by threatening to withhold funding from banks – a threat that was carried out in Greece in July 2015.

Meanwhile, on the other side of the Atlantic, the Fed continued to do QE, while elected politicians argued about whether they were going to honour spending commitments made by the President. The shenanigans about the 'debt ceiling' were not only embarrassing, they created uncertainty that helped to dampen the US recovery.

Japan seemed, briefly, to be an exception: after the election of Shinzo Abe as Prime Minister, the Bank of Japan and the Japanese government together embarked on an aggressive programme of monetary and fiscal stimulus, popularly dubbed 'Abenomics'. This was designed to lift the Japanese economy out of its decades-long slump and raise inflation off the floor. But then, in 2014 – encouraged by the IMF, which was becoming concerned about Japan's enormous public debt pile – the Japanese government raised sales taxes from five to eight per cent. The tax did increase inflation, temporarily. But not because people were spending more. On the contrary, it was because the tax itself raised prices. In response, people cut spending, and economic growth slumped. Once the temporary inflationary effect of the tax rise had worked its way out, inflation was back on the floor, along with growth.

The Great Experiment failed because of a subtle change in the way in which governments and central banks used helicopter money. In Friedman's cash-based world, the central bank prints the money, but the helicopter's flight path determines where that money falls, and it is government that flies the helicopter. Similarly, in Bernanke's world, the central bank's asset purchases enable governments to put more money into people's pockets. The money-financed tax cut that Bernanke describes as being equivalent to Friedman's 'helicopter drop' is both a monetary and a fiscal measure. The central bank provides the money, and the fiscal authority distributes it.

However, in the Great Experiment, central banks flew the helicopters as well as printing money. And they did so despite governments blowing them in the wrong direction. Somehow, 'a determined government' morphed into 'a determined central bank'. Friedman's 'helicopter drop' came not to mean putting money in people's pockets, but rather casting money blindly onto international financial markets without regard to where it would end up. Meanwhile, governments took money from ordinary people through tax rises and government spending cuts. It is hardly surprising that a tax rise squashed Japan's fragile economic recovery. What is surprising is that the rest of the world took no notice, but blindly continued with misguided austerity offset by ineffective QE.

Much of the developed world now seems to have followed Japan into the Long Stagnation. Despite repeated 'helicopter drops' over the last decade, interest rates are on the floor, debt levels remain high, and neither sustainable growth nor inflation has returned. How on earth did we end up here?

The Great Experiment

We are all Japan now

Modern central banking emerged from the high inflation of the 1970s and 1980s. Whether or not the central bank has an explicit inflation target (most do, these days), inflation dominates central bank forecasting and policymaking. The day after Lehman failed, the Federal Open Market Committee (FOMC) – the Federal Reserve's monetary policy committee – considered raising US interest rates because of fears of inflation.[20] The damage that the collapse of Lehman would do to the economy was simply off the radar.

At the time of the crisis, the prevailing belief among economists and politicians was that a determined central bank could always raise inflation, even if an equally determined government were simultaneously squeezing the private sector dry in the name of fiscal consolidation. There was also a general belief, almost amounting to a sacred cow, that governments cannot be trusted not to pursue inflationary fiscal policies, and that central banks must therefore be independent of political control if they are to prevent inflation from taking off. Early 1980s research papers, such as Sargent and Wallace's 'Some Unpleasant Monetarist Arithmetic', created frightening pictures of profligate governments going on spending sprees, thus sparking a rate of inflation that central banks would be quite unable to control.[21] No one ever thought that governments might become so wedded to cost-cutting that they would impede central banks' ability to raise inflation off the floor in a slump.

For a modern Western central bank, the primary aim of QE is to raise consumer price index (CPI) inflation. Inflation is defined as a rise in the general price level of goods and services in the economy. As economic energy returned, stimulated by the influx of new money, people would spend more, businesses would produce more, and people would demand – and get – higher wages. As a result, prices would rise.

Central banks saw the principal risk from QE as overdoing it. Monetary policy famously has 'long and variable lags', so the effects of QE could take some time to feed through into higher inflation. And money creation can go too far. Central banks feared a return to the wage–price spirals and stagflation of the 1970s, when too much money chased too few goods and services, causing annual CPI inflation to rise into double digits. It was perhaps understandable that central banks were worried about runaway inflation. The sheer scale of the Great Experiment was extraordinary. All around the world, an unprecedented quantity of new money was being created, and no one knew when it would end.

Furthermore, there is an even greater risk from money creation. If people start doubting that money will hold its value, they dump it as fast as they can. They buy gold, other precious metals, other financial assets, other currencies, art, fine wines, white goods, furnishings, and at the extreme even basics such as food and drink. Dumping the currency causes prices to rise faster and faster. This phenomenon is known as 'hyperinflation', and it is rightly feared. The iconic example of hyperinflation is the Weimar republic in Germany after the First World War. At its height, prices were rising by 29,000 per cent per annum, and people used wheelbarrows to transport paper notes.[22]

People feared that Friedman's helicopters would lead inevitably to Weimar's wheelbarrows. From the very start of QE, there were dark warnings that it would end in disaster. 'Hyperinflation is coming!' cried right-wing commentators. Government bond yields rose, as investors moved their money to 'safer' havens, notably gold and commodities.

Initially, central banks responded to all this fear, uncertainty and doubt by using QE sparingly and with a clear exit plan. In the first two rounds of

Federal Reserve QE, both the quantity of money to be created and the timespan over which it would be created were fixed in advance. The Bank of England, too, limited both the size and the timespan of QE purchases. And the ECB, worried that QE would violate the EU's legal restrictions on central bank financing of governments, didn't use QE at all until 2015, preferring to rely on providing direct support to banks. But not only did hyperinflationary Armageddon fail to materialize, even ordinary inflation disappointed. Economists reminded everyone about 'long and variable lags' and insisted that inflation would return 'any day now'. But as time went on, their predictions looked increasingly unreliable. Despite the largest money creation programme in history, inflation remained stubbornly below target in most developed countries.

Numerous reasons have been given for QE's failure to raise inflation. Damaged banks not lending, over-indebted borrowers not wanting banks to lend, low interest rates depriving savers of income, weak central banks too scared to do enough QE to make a difference, government deficits crowding out the private sector – all have been suggested. Some, including me, wondered whether, rather than causing inflation, QE was actually deflationary.[23] But there is a perfectly simple explanation for the failure of QE to raise CPI inflation significantly. It is all about where the helicopters fly.

Where the helicopters fly

HSBC's chief economist, Stephen King, commented on Twitter that QE had 'unfortunate distributional consequences'. He was right. QE has massively inflated asset prices. Stocks, bonds, commodities, oil, property, even art and fine wines – all of them have been pumped up by central bank money, directly benefiting the holders of those assets, who are mostly rich.[24]

Does this matter? If rich people buy new yachts, the makers of yachts benefit. If rich people buy art, artists benefit. If rich people buy corporate bonds or stocks, companies benefit, and that feeds through into more jobs and better wages for ordinary people. Spending by rich people should 'trickle down' to ordinary people, one way or another. But distributing money to the rich is nowhere near as powerful a stimulus to spending as giving ordinary people money. This is because the rich don't need the money. What economists call their 'marginal propensity to spend' is very low. In plain English, this means that if you give a rich person an additional dollar, they are unlikely to spend it, as they already have enough dollars to buy everything they want.

What the rich did with the money they received from QE was to buy assets. Admittedly, many of the assets they purchased were stocks and bonds. But they didn't necessarily buy the stocks and bonds of domestic companies. Much of the QE money went to buy sovereign and corporate bonds from emerging markets, which paid higher interest rates than domestic corporate bonds. And even when they did buy domestic bonds, those companies didn't necessarily invest the money productively. Many companies took the opportunity to buy back their own shares, rather than investing in plant and machinery, hiring and training more people, or raising wages to attract people with better skills.

The rich also bought property, fuelling price bubbles in prime city centre real estate around the world. Art, fine wine and antiques markets also hit unprecedented highs. And – worst of all – so did commodities. The huge rise in oil and commodity prices during the period of Federal Reserve QE, 2010–2014, raised the prices of essential energy and foodstuffs.[25]

The money created from QE didn't go to ordinary people to help them accommodate the rising cost of energy and food. No helicopters flew over Main Street. So people cut back non-essential spending. When price falls in non-essential items offset price rises in essentials, CPI doesn't move. The rising price of energy squeezed household incomes instead of raising CPI inflation.

In developing countries, the effect was even more unfortunate. Oil price rises due to QE combined with adverse weather conditions to cause sharp rises in the prices of essential foodstuffs. High food prices caused riots across Africa[26] and helped to trigger the Arab Spring, a series of uprisings across North Africa and the Middle East.[27]

There was another effect too. Very low interest rates encouraged investors to buy riskier assets in the hope of higher returns, a practice known as 'reach for yield'. One of the higher-risk asset classes that investors bought was bonds issued by governments and corporations in developing countries, mostly denominated in US dollars. The second and third rounds of Federal Reserve QE in particular were substantially invested in developing country assets. Marcel Fratzscher et al. estimated that QE increased the size of investment flows into developing country equity by over ten per cent.[28]

Inflows of money into developing countries pushed up currency exchange rates along with the prices of stocks, bonds and property. But this was not the patient long-term foreign direct investment that helps developing countries achieve sustainable growth. No, it was 'hot' money, which can depart as quickly as it arrives, leaving a trail of economic carnage. And depart it did, when the Federal Reserve turned off the QE taps in 2014–15. Oil and commodity markets crashed, along with the currency exchange rates of oil and commodity producing countries. Admittedly, the crash was partly due to falling demand for commodities as China's vast post-crisis investment declined. But ending QE was a contributory factor.

The large dollar reserves that many developing countries had built up helped to protect them from the worst of the crash, but those that tried to resist the depreciation of their currencies quickly found themselves running out of dollars. In parallel with the currency carnage, developing country stock and bond prices collapsed as investors diverted 'hot money' to safer havens such as US and Japanese stocks and bonds. Some oil exporters, such as Russia and Kazakhstan, floated their currencies, preferring high inflation to economic collapse. Others, notably Nigeria, Angola and Venezuela, suffered financial and economic crises.

Ten years after the fall of Lehman Brothers, the

Fed is now withdrawing QE, gradually shrinking its balance sheet. But, at the time of writing, the Bank of Japan is still actively purchasing assets, and both the Bank of England and the ECB are sitting on piles of government bonds, quietly reinvesting them when they mature so that the piles don't shrink. Interest rates across the developed world remain abnormally low, and growth in many countries is lacklustre. The Great Experiment may have warded off a Depression, but it has not restored the world to health. Instead of creating prosperity, governments and central banks have engendered economic stagnation.

2

Understanding Money

The failure of the Great Experiment was, in large part, because economists and central bankers misunderstood the nature of money and the role of the banking system. To understand why they got it so wrong, we need to look at how money and banking work in a modern economy.

What do we mean by 'money'?[1]

In a modern economy, almost all money in circulation is some form of credit. Credit money takes two principal forms:

- Banknotes and coins
- Electronic money

Of these, the second is by far the largest in modern advanced economies. According to the Bank of England, only three per cent of money in circulation in the UK is notes and coins created by, respectively, the Bank of England and the Royal Mint.[2] The rest is electronic money, mostly in commercial bank accounts. In modern economies, nearly all money in circulation is created by commercial banks.

Bank reserves are a special kind of money created by central banks to enable commercial banks to make payments. They are denominated in the same unit of account as notes and coins, but they circulate only between commercial and central banks. They can be exchanged for notes and coins at an exchange rate of 1:1. Commercial banks hold reserves in deposit accounts at the central bank, and lend them to each other via what is known as the 'interbank market'. In days gone by, bank reserves were in gold or banknotes, but these days they are electronic.

For the purposes of this book, 'money' will be taken to mean notes, coins and digital money created by central banks, together with electronic money created by commercial banks.

Box 2.1. Matryoshka money

Central banks record several different measures of money, or 'M'. Like a Russian 'matryoshka' doll – a series of dolls each of which fits inside the next, larger one – each measure of money fits inside the next, wider one.

M0 is 'base money' or the 'monetary base', sometimes known as 'outside money'. It is the money created by central banks, or – in days gone by – governments. M0 is divided into two parts: physical currency in circulation, and bank reserves.

M1 is what most people regard as money, namely the money in their current (checking) accounts and in their wallets. It does not include bank reserves, because bank reserves are not 'in circulation'.

M2 is M1 plus short-term savings accounts and overnight money market funds.

M3 is M2 plus long-term savings accounts and money market funds with a maturity longer than twenty-four hours.

M4 is M3 plus other deposits.

M1 to M4 are collectively known as 'broad money' or 'inside money'. All broad money, except legal tender notes and coins, is created by commercial banks.

How commercial banks create money

Commercial banks create 'inside money', also known as 'broad money' or M1, when they lend. Bank lending is the source of nearly all the money in circulation in the economy. The fact that banks create money when they lend is not a 'right' or a 'privilege' granted by government to regulated banks. It inevitably arises from combining double entry accounting with the measures of money described above.

In order to understand this, consider a bank making a new mortgage loan to a young couple, Bob and Mary. They have seen a house they want to buy, and they know how much it will cost. They contribute some funds of their own, amounting to ten per cent of the purchase price, and the rest is provided by the bank against the security of the house they are buying. They will make regular payments of interest and principal to the bank for the next twenty-five years. If they default on those payments, the bank will have the right to seize the house and sell it to recover the money it has loaned. This is simple long-term secured lending. Thousands of such loans are agreed every day in modern economies. And every single one creates new money.

How does it do this? When the loan is agreed, the bank makes a balanced pair of accounting entries. It creates a new loan asset for the amount of the loan, and it credits the young couple's demand deposit account with the amount of the loan:

DR – Bob and Mary's loan account
CR – Bob and Mary's demand deposit (checking or 'current') account

Both of these entries are made 'from thin air'. No money is transferred from any other accounts at this point. Thus, since M1 measures money in demand deposit accounts at commercial banks, the accounting entries for the loan increase M1 by the amount of the loan. This is how commercial banks create money.

Unfortunately, many descriptions of bank lending in economics textbooks give the impression that banks lend out existing money (deposits or reserves). This is because they conflate lending with payments. Payments from bank deposit accounts are made with money that already exists. The bank simply transfers money, rather than creating it. This is true even if the payment is the draw-down of a loan. The bank creates money when it approves the loan, then transfers it when the loan is drawn.

So, when Bob and Mary complete their house purchase – which might be several weeks after the bank has agreed the loan – they pay the total amount of the loan to the seller, together with the ten per cent of the selling price that they are contributing from their own savings. To make the payment, the bank debits the whole amount (loan plus savings) from their demand deposit account, and transfers money from its own reserve account to the seller's bank's reserve account.

Bob and Mary's bank
DR – Bob and Mary's demand deposit account
CR – reserve account

House seller's bank
DR – reserve account
CR – house seller's demand deposit account

Central bank
DR – Bob and Mary's bank's reserve account
CR – house seller's bank's reserve account

This series of accounting entries is an interbank transfer. It simply transfers to another bank money that was created some weeks before. Even if payment happens immediately after lending, the money transferred already exists, because it was created when the loan was agreed. All bank lending results in new money being created as described above.

New money is similarly created when a bank buys securities or other assets.

Economic models of lending that imply that banks lend out money they already have are unable to explain satisfactorily how M1 expands with lending. They may recognize a relationship between bank lending and M1 growth, but they are likely to suggest that bank lending increases because M1 is growing. Often, this is mistakenly put down to increased saving. In fact, M1 grows because bank lending increases, not the other way round, and any increased saving arises from the higher spending that is usually a consequence of rising bank lending. In a modern economy, because nearly all money in circulation is commercial bank credit, it is only possible for people to save if other people take on debt.

The misrepresentation of bank lending so prevalent in economics textbooks can have unfortunate consequences for economic policy. Increased saving by households and businesses does not result in increased bank lending, and it cannot increase M1. On the contrary, since people borrow to spend, bank lending is likely to fall if households and businesses prefer to save rather than spend. Since M1 reduces when bank loans are paid off, and loans are being paid off all the time, falling bank lending tends to reduce M1. Thus, economic policies that encourage saving in the mistaken belief that it will spur bank lending actually tend to reduce bank lending and diminish money in circulation.

The real role of bank reserves

Bank reserves are not included in measures of money 'in circulation'. But they are crucial for the operation of the payments system: without them, today's fast, efficient electronic payments could not be made. And they are also essential for the transmission of central bank monetary policy.

As the accounting entries for Bob and Mary's house purchase in the previous section show, when a bank customer makes an electronic payment to a customer of a different bank, the sending bank debits the customer's account and the receiving bank credits the payee's account. But for the payment to transfer, there must be balancing entries in the banks' reserve accounts, too. So the central bank debits the sending bank's reserve account and credits the receiving bank's reserve account.

If the sending bank doesn't have enough reserves to make the payment, it must fund the account. Some central banks set a minimum reserve requirement: the Federal Reserve, for example, sets a minimum reserve of ten per cent for American banks. Others, such as the Canadian Central Bank, have no reserve requirement. Banks subject to a reserve requirement must fund their reserve accounts when forthcoming payments will take the balance below the required level. Banks not subject to a reserve requirement must fund them if forthcoming payments would force the account into deficit. Banks fund their reserve accounts by borrowing from other banks on the interbank market or, as a last resort, from the central bank itself. When the central bank lends reserves to a bank, it creates new reserves, so the total quantity of reserves in circulation increases.

As well as lending to banks, central banks also create or destroy reserves by means of asset purchases and sales: buying assets from the private sector creates new reserves, while selling assets to the private sector destroys them. Asset purchases and sales that adjust the total quantity of reserves are known as 'Open Market Operations' (OMO). Central banks can use OMOs to offset ('sterilize') the expansionary effect of lending new reserves to individual banks, so that the total quantity of reserves in circulation remains the same.

Thus, the central bank controls the total quantity of reserves available to banks. But it does not determine the quantity of reserves each bank holds, even if there is a minimum reserve requirement. The quantity of reserves each bank holds depends on the pattern of payments and deposits, the bank's own reserve policy (does it want to hold excess reserves to cover eventualities, or just rely on market funding being available?) and the interest rates banks charge each other to borrow reserves.

Prior to the financial crisis, influencing (but not directly setting) the interbank lending rate was a pillar of central bank monetary policy. But the interbank market now is very different from the market prior to the financial crisis. In large part, this is due to QE. By creating enormous quantities of bank reserves – far more than banks needed to settle payments – it fundamentally changed the way central bank monetary policy works. These days, banks have much less need for interbank borrowing, because the total quantity of reserves in circulation is far more than they need, and collectively they must hold all the reserves the central bank issues. So the dominant interest rate now is not the rate at which banks will lend to each other, but the rate that the central bank will pay on money deposited with it. This situation will not change while the excess reserves created by QE remain in the system.

The shortcomings of bank-created money

The problem with relying on bank lending to create the money people use for their everyday purchases is that bank lending is not steady. When times are good and people feel optimistic about the future, they will borrow to spend: but when times are hard and the future looks worse, people pay off debt and are reluctant to borrow any more, preferring to 'live within their means' and save for the future. This may be encouraged by government policy. Similarly, banks will lend when times are good and the future is rosy, because they are confident about getting their money back; but when the storm clouds gather, banks reduce lending and may call in existing loans. Thus, the supply of broad money in the economy tends to increase when the economy is booming and decrease in a downturn.

These money supply swings are amplified dramatically in a major financial or economic crisis. In a financial crisis, bank lending can stop completely, and there may be widespread loan defaults. Loan defaults and early redemptions destroy credit money, and when banks aren't lending, that money is not replaced. Thus, in an economic crisis, the supply of money to the economy can fall drastically. Figure 2.1 shows how bank lending in

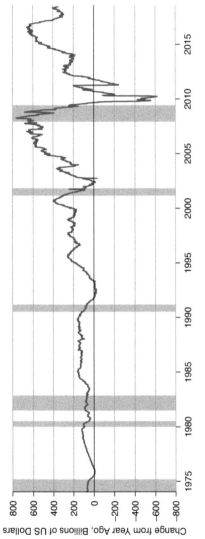

Figure 2.1. Loans and leases in bank credit, all commercial banks Shaded areas indicate US recessions.

Source: Board of Governors of the US Federal Reserve System.

the US collapsed during the Great Recession of 2008–2009.[3]

Figure 2.2 shows how the growth rate of broad money (M2) correspondingly fell, though not to zero as might have been expected from the scale of the bank lending collapse.[4] Why did broad money hold up when bank lending was collapsing? The answer is QE. QE replaces lost commercial bank credit money with newly created central bank money. So, the chart shows that the Federal Reserve's QE maintained the stock of broad money when banks stopped lending. By way of comparison, Figure 2.3 shows the growth rate of broad money in the Eurozone 2008–2009, where the ECB didn't do QE at this time.[5] Without QE, the growth rate of broad money fell to zero.

How QE maintains the money supply

Putting new money into the economy supports spending and investment, thus preventing a crisis turning into a Depression as it did in 1929–33. The US was the source of the 2008 crisis and experienced the worst banking crash. Yet it recovered much more quickly than the Eurozone. Many economists attribute this to the Federal Reserve's

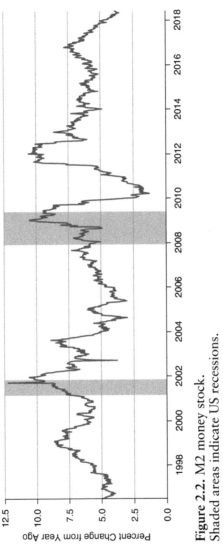

Figure 2.2. M2 money stock.
Shaded areas indicate US recessions.

Source: Board of Governors of the US Federal Reserve System.

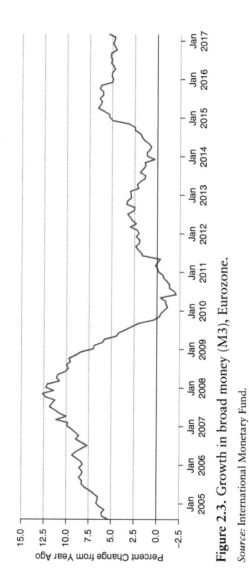

Figure 2.3. Growth in broad money (M3), Eurozone.

Source: International Monetary Fund.

extensive use of one particular form of QE. Between 2008 and 2014, the Federal Reserve poured $4.6tn of new money into the US economy using what are known as 'large-scale asset purchases' (LSAPs).

Large-scale asset purchases

LSAPs are similar to Open Market Operations, but on a much larger scale. The central bank buys assets from the private sector, paying for them with newly created central bank money. When people talk about QE, they usually mean LSAPs. If the assets are bought directly from banks, then the only new money created is bank reserves (M0). But if the assets are bought from non-banks, such as pension funds and corporations, both M0 and M1 (bank deposits) increase. This is because the central bank pays for the securities it purchases by crediting the sellers' bank accounts.

When a new deposit is made at a commercial bank, double entry accounting requires that there be a new asset as well, namely a corresponding increase in the bank's reserves at the central bank. However, a new deposit at a commercial bank is normally made by transferring funds from another commercial bank, either directly or via banknotes and coins. For example, when Mary's employer pays her salary, the increase in her bank account balance is exactly matched by a reduction in her employer's bank account balance. Thus, one bank's new deposit is another bank's deposit withdrawal. The reserve accounts reflect this: the reserve increase at Mary's bank that corresponds to the new deposit is matched by a reserve decrease at her employer's bank. The overall quantity of reserves in the system doesn't change.

However, when the central bank pays for asset purchases from non-banks by crediting their bank accounts, only one commercial bank is involved. There is no reserve transfer from another commercial bank. Instead, the central bank creates new reserves. Thus, the seller's deposit balance (M1) increases by the amount of the sale, and their bank's reserve balance (M0) also increases by the same amount. Most central banks have purchased assets from both banks and non-banks. QE has therefore resulted in a very large increase in both inside money (M1) and the bank reserves component of outside money (M0). The increase in outside money from three rounds of Federal Reserve LSAPs, in 2008–2009, 2011 and 2013–2014, can be clearly seen in Figure 2.4.

Most LSAPs involve purchases of government debt. Some central banks also buy corporate debt and one (the Bank of Japan) buys some corporate

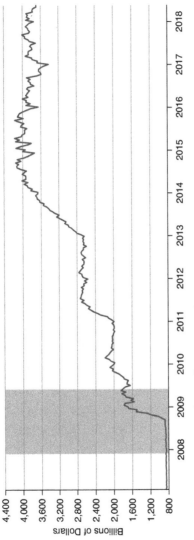

Figure 2.4. St Louis adjusted monetary base.
Shaded areas indicate US recessions.

Source: Federal Reserve Bank of St Louis.

equities. Central banks that are doing LSAPs to prevent their currency exchange rate rising, as for example the Swiss National Bank did during the Eurozone crisis, usually buy foreign currencies and/ or foreign governments' debt (which is a future claim on their currency). The effect of LSAPs on the broad and base money supply is the same regardless of the type of asset purchased. However, the economic effects may differ widely. Where the new money goes is every bit as important as how much is created. Indeed, it may be even more important.

Other forms of QE
Central banks used other types of QE to encourage corporations and households to borrow, and banks to lend. For example, in 'Operation Twist', the Federal Reserve bought long-dated US Treasuries and sold short-term Treasury bills. Increasing the supply of short-dated bonds reduced their market price, while reducing the supply of long-dated bonds increased their market price. The yield on bonds is the inverse of the price, and the interest rate on new issues relates to the yield on bonds already in circulation. Thus, increasing the price of long-term debt reduced the interest rate on newly issued bonds.

The immediate beneficiary of this was the US government, which was able to issue long-term debt at lower interest rates. But, because the yield on corporate debt is determined by the yield on US Treasuries plus a risk premium, lowering US Treasury yields also lowered the yields on corporate debt. This encouraged large corporations to issue new debt. The Fed expected that higher corporate borrowing would result in more capital investment, generating jobs and increasing economic activity.

The reality was disappointing. Corporations did increase bond issuance, but they spent the money on buying back shares, flattering their returns on equity and giving shareholders windfalls without significantly increasing productive activity. The lesson of Operation Twist is that throwing money at corporations doesn't make them invest productively. Risk-averse corporations facing a gloomy economic outlook don't borrow to expand. They batten down the hatches and wait for better times. Central banks also threw money at banks in the hope that they would lend more, which would increase broad money supply and help to kick-start growth. For example, during the Eurozone crisis, the ECB did a series of 'long-term repo operations' (LTROs), which provided banks with cheap funding in return for pledged assets, principally government bonds.

Banks lend when the returns justify the risks. But in the aftermath of the 2008 financial crisis, regulators pressured banks to reduce risks, while low interest rates reduced banks' returns. So, far from increasing lending, banks reduced it. Cheap lending helped to prevent a banking system meltdown, but it didn't kick-start growth.

Why QE didn't work

Ten years after the financial crisis, unemployment remains elevated in many countries; in others, low unemployment has been bought at the expense of wage growth and living standards. The returns on all that new money created for the benefits of big banks and big corporations seem to be extremely poor. Asset price rises have inflated the wealth of the rich, but small businesses and ordinary people continue to suffer from a crippling lack of money. Somehow, the mechanism for distributing money to the economy has broken down. What has gone wrong?

The problem is that central banks don't deal directly with the real economy. They deal only with banks and financial markets. They provide the money that banks need to make payments.

They intervene in financial markets to support asset prices and currency exchange rates. But they don't directly support small and medium-size enterprises or households. And now that governments in many countries have written into law a prohibition on central bank financing of government spending, they don't support governments either. Their job is to keep the wheels spinning in the financial centres, not to ensure that money gets to those who need it.

But if central banks and governments can't distribute money to ordinary people, who can? The only source of new money for the real economy is commercial banks. If they don't want to lend – or if already indebted firms and households don't want to borrow – no new money gets into circulation. Wall Street is awash with public money, while Main Street dies of thirst. This, in a nutshell, is what has gone wrong since 2008. Damaged commercial banks, under pressure from governments to make themselves safer so that bailouts would become a thing of the past, have reduced lending seen as 'risky' – which unfortunately includes lending to small and medium-size businesses, the productive engines of the economy. Households, suffering from high unemployment and stagnating incomes, have paid off (or defaulted on) their debts and refused to borrow any more. Corporations, worried about future sales prospects and the parlous state of their own balance sheets, have bought back their shares and refinanced their debts at artificially low rates, instead of investing for the future. And governments, scared by rising debt, have harshly cut back government programmes that supported the poor and vulnerable, causing their incomes to crash. Meanwhile, the money created by QE has churned around on financial markets and blown up asset bubbles all over the world.

There is a better way. Central banks and governments can intervene directly in the economy, putting funding into capital investment and money into ordinary people's pockets. This is QE for the People.

3

QE for the People:
A Better Way

What is QE for the People?

In 2012, the economist John Muellbauer wrote an article entitled 'QE for the People', in which he proposed that the ECB should distribute 500 euros per person to all EU citizens.[1] At the time, Muellbauer's idea attracted little attention. But the seed had been sown. Since then, many economists have proposed versions of 'QE for the People'. In the EU, there is now a pressure group campaigning for 'QE for the People'.[2] And in the UK, a 'People's QE' scheme briefly became the opposition Labour Party's official policy. QE for the People simply restores Friedman's helicopters to their rightful role. Instead of flying solely over Wall Street, they can fly over the whole economy, delivering money to wherever it is most needed via a variety of channels.

QE for the People: A Better Way

'QE for the People' proposals fall broadly into two groups:

- Those that involve giving money directly to people to boost spending in the short term
- Those that involve longer-term investment to achieve some sort of rebalancing of the economy

Although campaigners for different forms of 'QE for the People' often dismiss competing ideas, the two groups can be complementary.

QE for the People, type 1: Give the People the money

This is what most people mean by 'helicopter money'. It is a short-term monetary boost to kick-start economic growth by giving people more spending power. This sort of 'QE for the People' would work in the immediate aftermath of a financial shock before it has started to cause serious damage to the economy's supply side. It would support retail spending and prevent widespread debt defaults by homeowners and small businesses. Replacing 'QE for the Banks' with this type of 'QE for the People' is economically attractive. Supporting Wall

QE for the People: A Better Way

Street failed to prevent the deepest recession since the 1930s. Had homeowners and small businesses received the level of support that banks and large corporations did, the Great Recession might have been merely a minor economic downturn.

'QE for the People' is politically attractive too. There was widespread popular anger about governments and central banks pouring money into financial markets while ordinary people lost their homes and their jobs. Initially, that anger was mainly expressed against banks, for instance through the Occupy protests. But now, people are turning their anger against economic 'experts', central banks, and centrist politicians. Politics is polarizing: the centre ground previously occupied by mainstream political parties is hollowing out, and popular opinion is shifting to extremes, both on the right and the left. Populist politicians on right and left alike now promote a nationalist and protectionist agenda which threatens the international legal and institutional framework painstakingly constructed since the Second World War. Had QE for the People been the policy choice during the Great Recession, the resurgence of destructive nationalism might have been avoided.

However, supporting asset prices and preventing banks from failing did protect many ordinary people. In the US and UK, allowing financial asset prices to collapse would wipe out the savings of millions of savers and retirees. And in Europe, where savings tend to be kept in banks rather than invested on capital markets, allowing banks to fail would similarly wipe out the savings of ordinary people. The social costs of allowing financial markets to crash and banks to fail can be very high: in 2016, four small Italian banks were forcibly wound up, wiping the life savings of elderly Italians. One of them committed suicide.[3]

Of course, banks can be nationalized and savers can be compensated. But helicopter money would do neither of those. So perhaps 'QE for the People' should be seen as a complement to central bank and government support for financial markets and banks, rather than a replacement for it. Let QE go to **all** the people, including those who rely on savings.

I will now discuss the forms that this type of QE for the People can take.

1. Helicopter drops

Friedman's 'helicopter drop' is a form of short-term demand stimulus. Friedman insisted that the helicopter should only fly once. In practice the helicopters might fly more than once, if the recession is deep, but they should not need to continue flying forever. Of course, these days, no one would drop bank notes from helicopters. In developed countries, most people have bank accounts. The central bank can simply credit bank accounts. Alternatively, the central bank could send a cheque to every individual.

Many people have more than one bank account, however. How would the central bank ensure that each individual only received one payment? Some kind of authentication would be needed. Furthermore, about eight per cent of the population in developed countries do not have bank accounts. These people include some of the poorest in society – homeless people, for example – for whom a bank account is impossible because they have no fixed address. Excluding them from the helicopter drop would be unfair. It would also reduce its effectiveness, since these are the people most likely to spend the money rather than save it.

One way for the central bank to deliver one-off helicopter money might be for every individual to have an account at the central bank. The central bank would simply credit these accounts according to need. An alternative might be to issue prepaid cards which would be accepted by retailers.

There have been several proposals concerning the extension of central bank accounts to ordinary people and businesses. Most of these aim to disintermediate banks and end their ability to create credit money, thus giving central banks complete control of the creation of money even in stable times. But this would not be 'helicopter money'. The essence of helicopter drops is that they are one-offs.

In developing countries, far fewer people have bank accounts, and distributing physical cash could be both difficult and dangerous. One promising channel for distributing helicopter money in developing countries is via mobile phones, to which a significant proportion of people have access. It might be necessary to use multiple distribution channels to ensure that as many people as possible receive the money. However, it is not necessary for absolutely everyone to receive money. What matters is that a high proportion of the population does receive money, and that the majority of people spend it. Helicopter money distribution could be specifically targeted at the poor, who are more likely to spend the money than the rich.

One way or another, it should be possible for the central bank to give a sufficient number of people a one-off payment in order to provide a short-term economic boost to the economy. As the money would be distributed directly to people rather than given to the government, it would not breach prohibitions on central bank financing of governments. This type of 'QE for the People' could therefore be implemented by any central bank.

2. *Financing government deficits*

From an economic perspective, Bernanke's idea of a money-financed tax cut is equivalent to Friedman's helicopter drop. But it works entirely differently. Instead of the central bank giving money to people, it would give it to the government, which would distribute it to people in the form of tax cuts (or welfare payments, for those who are too poor to pay tax).

There are three principal ways of doing a central bank-financed tax cut and/or welfare payment.

- The central bank could lend money to the government, either as a loan or in the form of an overdraft account such as the Bank of England's 'ways and means' facility. As the central bank is an arm of government, the loan would be 'off the books' as far as the government was concerned.
- The government could issue bonds, which the central bank would buy. The central bank's purchases could form part of a conventional QE programme, in which case the central bank

would buy the bonds from investors and banks after the initial issue. Alternatively, the central bank could buy the initial issue itself.

- The government could issue bonds which domestic banks would buy and then pledge at the central bank as collateral for funding. This device was used by several Eurozone countries during the 2011–2013 crisis.

The second and third of these would increase the government's deficit and the stock of government debt, though the first would not. However, as the economy recovered, tax revenue would increase, and the loan, overdraft or bonds would gradually be paid off.

Central bank financing of government deficits by means of loans, overdrafts and purchases of primary issues of bonds is currently illegal in many countries. However, purchasing bonds in the secondary market is a standard part of central bank monetary operations and QE, while pledging government bonds is the primary means by which banks fund themselves. One way or another, therefore, central banks could finance government distribution of helicopter money.

3. *Debt jubilee*

This category is included because the immediate effect of a debt jubilee would be to boost spending. People relieved of the burden of debt would be very likely to buy goods and services that they have been unable to afford because of the constant income drain due to debt service. It would be the equivalent of a helicopter drop.

In their book 'House of Debt', Mian and Sufi showed how subprime adjustable-rate mortgage borrowers cut back hard on spending when interest rates rose in 2006, triggering house price falls.[4] People who had been borrowing against the equity in their homes to fund spending suddenly found themselves with more debt than their home was worth: other people who might have borrowed against equity to fund spending were suddenly unable to do so. So, consumer spending fell sharply across the economy, causing widespread business failures and job losses. This in turn fed the consumer spending collapse, which was then exacerbated by a very large rise in fuel prices shortly before the failure of Lehman Brothers. Had the Fed or the US government written off some or all household debts, people might not have cut spending so hard, and the deep recession of 2009 could have been avoided.

Writing off debts would also have long-term structural effects. In Western economies today, private debt levels are very high. This limits the ability of banks to create the money that a growing economy needs, and increases the likelihood of another damaging debt deflationary crisis. There is a strong argument that reducing the general level of private debt would give the economy room to grow.

However, debt jubilee has some serious difficulties. Relieving debt distress among banks and corporations costs taxpayers billions of dollars. Relieving debt distress among mortgage holders could cost the same. It is difficult to see why a young person on a low income who is struggling to pay their rent should, through their taxes, pay off the million-dollar mortgage of a business tycoon. It is also hard to see why homeowners who limit their borrowing to what they can sensibly afford should receive less from the government than people who mortgage themselves to the hilt in the expectation that house prices will always rise. Debt jubilee could be very unfair to people who are too poor to have debts or too responsible to over-borrow.

There is a second problem with debt jubilee. For every debtor, there is a creditor; and creditors are savers. Writing off debts therefore means writing down the value of savings. But working hard and building up savings is widely regarded as virtuous. Imposing losses on people who have saved, to write off the debts of those who have not, would be very unfair. Somehow, a debt jubilee would have to avoid hurting savers.

One way of addressing these problems might be for debt jubilee to take the form of a central bank helicopter drop rather than a government bailout. In this version of a helicopter drop, the money would be used in the first instance to pay down debts. Any money left over after debts were discharged would be given directly to the individual: they could either spend the money or add it to their savings. If the amount of money dropped was insufficient to discharge the debt, the individual would still have to pay the balance and interest over time, but the debt service costs would obviously be lower.

QE for the People, type 2: Economic rebalancing

Many people have argued that, rather than central bank money financing a short-term spending boost in a depressed economy, such money should be used to bring about lasting structural change in the economy. There are numerous proposals for central bank financing of long-term initiatives.

Box 3.1. Types of QE for the People.

Short-term stimulus

QE for the People	Muellbauer	500 euros to each adult Eurozone citizen
People's TLTRO	Lonergan	A payment to each adult Eurozone citizen (amount unspecified)
People's QE	Lonergan et al.	A payment to each British citizen (amount unspecified)
Helicopter money	Buiter	Temporary financing of government deficit spending
Money-financed tax cut	Bernanke	Temporary financing of increased government deficit due to tax cuts
Helicopter drop	Friedman	Undirected distribution of physical cash
Bounty hunt (semi-serious)	Keynes	Dig up bottles full of cash

Longer-term financing

Green QE	Murphy and Hines	Central bank (BoE) financing of green investments
People's QE	UK Labour Party	Central bank (BoE) financing of public infrastructure
Green money: Reclaiming QE	Anderson	Central bank (ECB) financing of green investments
Debt monetization	Turner	To support Japan's ageing population
Debt jubilee	Barnes and Kumhof	Mortgage loan write-off (part of Sovereign Money transition)
Debt jubilee	Keen	Private debt write-off (not limited to mortgages)
Juncker Plan	European Commission	Public/private investment via EIB, with the option for the ECB to monetize at need

QE for the People: A Better Way

Central bank financing of public investment is an attractive option when there are deep structural problems such as regional inequality, over-dependence on asset price rises and consumption for growth, and 'Dutch disease' (deindustrialization due to over-reliance on extractive industries such as oil). Arguably, financing public investment would have been a more effective way of getting Western economies out of their slump than QE2, QE3 or any of the other desperate measures central banks used to counteract the effects of fiscal austerity, raise inflation and restore growth.

There are two principal ways in which central banks can finance public investment: one is by directly financing government, and the other is by buying bonds issued by a state investment bank. Central banks can also directly support private sector investment, by buying corporate bonds and equities, and by supporting small and medium-size enterprises (SMEs).

1. Direct financing of government

This is similar to the financing of government deficit spending discussed above. The central bank can lend to the government, or it can buy bonds issued by the government. Bond issues could be bought either on issue, which would mean the central bank explicitly underwriting the issue, or from investors on the open market, perhaps as part of a standard QE programme.

As the purpose of the financing would be to support investment projects that could take years to complete, a central bank overdraft facility would not be an appropriate vehicle for this sort of lending. The central bank could make long-term loans instead. These might carry an interest rate somewhere between the market rate for government bonds of that tenor and the central bank's bank lending rate (Fed Funds Rate in the USA, Bank Rate in the UK). If the central bank is wholly government-owned (as it is in the UK), the loans could have an interest rate of zero, since this would really be a transfer between different parts of government. As they would not form part of the national debt, the government could (in theory) launch numerous public investment projects without fear of a buyer's strike.[5]

There is, however, a snag. I explained in Chapter 2 that in normal times the central bank controls inflation by adjusting the quantity of bank reserves in circulation so as to maintain a target interest rate on its own lending to banks. Bank reserves are the central bank's own liabilities so, in effect, the central bank controls inflation by adjusting the size of its own balance sheet. If 'QE for the People' were to leave a large number of long-term loans on the central bank's balance sheet, the central bank might find its ability to adjust the size of its balance sheet restricted, with possibly serious consequences for inflation.

One way of addressing this problem might be for the central bank to securitize the loans, i.e. issue its own bonds backed by the loans. This would withdraw reserves from circulation to the value of the loans, replacing them with bonds which could be bought or borrowed back at need to support monetary policy objectives. 'Sterilizing' the loans in this way would mean they were no longer 'helicopter money', strictly speaking, since the amount of money in circulation would not increase. But it would enable a central bank to finance public investment projects without losing control of inflation.

Bonds issued by the government for the purposes of financing investment projects would be separate from bonds issued to cover general financing needs. They might also be very long term – much longer than the duration of the projects themselves. Potentially, therefore, the central bank could hold these bonds for a very long time.

If the central bank were to buy the entire primary issue and hold it to maturity, the bonds would effectively be the same as term loans. They would be slightly more flexible, though, since they could be sold or loaned out at need to help the central bank meet its inflation target. If the central bank bought public investment bonds as part of a QE programme, they would be treated in exactly the same way as all other bonds purchased under the programme. They could be loaned out to meet monetary policy objectives, and they would eventually be sold back to the private sector.

2. National Investment Banks

Central banks can also finance public investment projects via National Investment Banks (NIBs). For countries that prohibit central bank financing of government, this could be a good way of providing central bank support for long-term public investment. The NIB would issue bonds to the market, which the central bank would buy either as part of a QE programme or simply in the course of day-to-day open market operations. As the NIB would be separate from government, the central bank could additionally buy part or all of a primary bond issue, which it could either hold to maturity or sell in the course of normal monetary operations. As with direct government financing, a large quantity of NIB bonds on the central bank's balance sheet could impede its ability to control inflation if there was a political expectation that the central bank would always keep NIB bond yields low.

3. Direct investment in private sector businesses

A central bank that buys the bonds of its own government, denominated in the currency that it issues, is taking no risks and picking no winners. But a central bank that is buying corporate bonds and equities is making decisions about the allocation of credit in the economy, and subsidizing private sector businesses. It is also taking credit risk (the risk that the borrower will default).

Central banks can be reluctant to invest directly in private sector businesses, not least because it exposes them to criticism regarding their portfolio choices. For example, eyebrows were raised when the Bank of England decided to buy Apple's bonds. Not only does Apple have absolutely no need of financial assistance from any central bank, it was at the time suffering heavy criticism for tax avoidance in the EU.[6] Central banks have also been criticized for buying the bonds of companies that contribute to global warming.[7]

It is also by no means clear that subsidizing large corporations by reducing their borrowing costs necessarily benefits the real economy. The companies that are more likely to suffer in a downturn are SMEs. These are the backbone of most economies and employ the largest number of people. It could be more beneficial for central banks to invest in SMEs rather than large corporations. The problem is how to do this. Central banks don't lend to non-banks, and SMEs don't generally issue bonds. Two possible solutions have been advanced:

1. Bundling and securitization of SME loans. The central bank could buy securities backed by bundles of SME loans.[8]
2. Term lending to SMEs. The central bank would need to create reserve accounts for SMEs. A big obstacle would be collateral: SMEs don't tend to have much in the way of financial assets they can pledge to obtain funds. Government might have to provide SMEs with guarantees (most governments already do this for some kinds of SME finance).

Another possibility, which would particularly support innovative startups, would be for the central bank to take equity stakes in some businesses. The problem with this is that the central bank would be doing 'stock picking', which is a risky active portfolio management strategy for which it would have neither the mandate nor the expertise. It would also open it to accusations of interfering with the operation of free markets and 'crony capitalism'. Rather than the central bank investing directly, therefore, it might be preferable for government to create a leveraged 'wealth fund', which would manage investment portfolios on behalf of the government, potentially including equity stakes in startups. This investment fund would issue bonds to fund its acquisitions, which the central bank could buy.

4

Some (Weak) Objections to QE for the People

The inflation chimera

Among economists and central bankers, and even among the general public, there is a widespread belief that the central bank doing helicopter drops and/or financing government spending would inevitably lead to hyperinflation. Money printing by the German central bank is often cited as the cause of the Weimar Republic's iconic hyperinflation.[1] But, less than a decade later, the Bank of Japan's money printing helped to restore the Japanese economy in the Great Depression. Japan left the gold standard towards the end of 1931 and embarked on a large programme of coordinated monetary and fiscal stimulus. The Bank of Japan cut interest rates by three per cent, and the yen depreciated by over fifty per cent. The government deficit, financed by bonds underwritten by the Bank of Japan, rose by five per cent of GDP.

Figures from the Bank of Japan show that the stimulus programme stopped the disastrous deflation of 1930–1931, when prices were falling at a rate of 10.3 per cent per annum. But it didn't cause significant inflation. During the period of the stimulus programme, inflation was low and stable at about 1.5 per cent per annum. Not until Japan started rearming in 1937 did inflation begin to rise.[2]

The three-pronged stimulus programme also brought about a remarkable recovery in the Japanese economy. Business profits soared, helped by an industrial policy that strengthened cartels. By 1933, the economy was growing at an extraordinary 10.1 per cent per annum.[3] Japan's experience shows that central bank financing of government deficits does not necessarily cause runaway inflation. We need to understand why Weimar experienced hyperinflation when Japan did not.

The Cato Institute documents all known instances of hyperinflation since the French Revolution, with – so far as can be established – their primary causes. In the twentieth century, there are three clusters of hyperinflations: the first was after the First World War (Germany was not the only country to experience hyperinflation at that time), the second was during and after the Second World War, and the third was after the fall of the Iron Curtain in 1989. There are also some individual country hyperinflations such as in Zimbabwe and, now, Venezuela.[4]

The Cato Institute researchers, Steve Hanke and Nicholas Krus, say that hyperinflation arises under extreme conditions, such as war, political mismanagement, and the transition from a command to market-based economy (this last explains the hyperinflations after the fall of the Iron Curtain). In his study of hyperinflation, Cullen Roche explains how the source of hyperinflation lies in existing economic conditions:

> What lays the groundwork for the hyperinflation is severe exogenous forces or a highly unusual environment that government either creates or responds to ineffectively or inappropriately. In sum, Weimar Republic was not merely a case of 'money printing' gone wild. In fact, it was the war, regime change, fragile state of mind, foreign denominated debts and productive collapse that resulted in the excessive 'money printing', collapse in the tax system and ultimately hyperinflation.[5]

Hyperinflation occurs when people lose confidence in the ability of the central bank to maintain the value of the money it issues. Otmar Issing, former

President of the Bundesbank, says that once central banks started giving people money, they would not be able to stop, and this would inevitably trigger a crisis of confidence which would destroy the value of money.[6] It's a frightening image. But it is not true. Hyperinflation is one hundred per cent associated with government ineptitude (or absence). There is no reason why money creation by a competent central bank cooperating with a responsible and trusted government should ever trigger hyperinflation.

In fact, the Great Experiment has taught us that central banks can create enormous amounts of money without triggering hyperinflation, if people believe they are in control of money creation. There is no reason why distributing that money to ordinary people instead of pouring it into financial markets should make hyperinflation inevitable. We also know that QE can be temporary, as Friedman envisaged. The Federal Reserve, the Bank of England and the Swiss National Bank had all stopped doing QE by the end of 2014. At the time of writing, the Federal Reserve is now actively reducing the size of its balance sheet. If central banks can stop doing QE for the Banks, and even reverse it, they can also stop doing QE for the People.

Japan's money creation in the 1930s was loudly criticized, particularly by American journalists. In

1932, Burton Crane, a correspondent for the *Wall Street Journal*, acidly commented: 'Financial leaders of Japan, assembled at the bank of Japan at the request of Korekiyo Takahashi, finance minister, recommended measures which they thought likely to help Japan in its present difficulties. The three measures suggested were (1) inflation, (2) inflation and (3) inflation.'[7] But it was America, not Japan, that suffered the most in the Great Depression. When fear of inflation prevents policymakers providing the money that people need, the result is misery.

For those who lived through the 1970s, the fear is not so much Weimar-style hyperinflation as 'stagflation' – high inflation coupled with low growth and rising unemployment. The stagflation of the 1970s was eventually broken by the Volcker Shock of 1981, when the Fed raised interest rates to an unprecedented twenty per cent. Interest rates stayed high throughout the 1980s as central banks gradually brought inflation under control. By the early 1990s, inflation was low and stable. Now, the prevailing belief is that inflation was tamed by inflation-targeting central banks independent of political control. Inflation targeting and central bank independence are thus the twin pillars of inflation control. They must be maintained at all costs to prevent the return of the inflation of the 1970s.

But anyone who had been paying attention to Japan in the 1990s would have known that central banks can't always control inflation. When a central bank has an inflation target, inflation far below the target is just as serious a failure as inflation running well above it. While other central banks were beginning to defeat inflation in the early 1990s, the Bank of Japan was already fighting deflation – and losing. Japan had an enormous real estate bubble in the 1980s, which burst catastrophically in 1990. The Bank of Japan cut interest rates to zero, to no avail. Economic growth failed to return, and deflation became entrenched.

Today, the Great Experiment has shown that no central bank knows how to fight deflation. Ten years after the financial crisis, inflation in most Western countries remains well below central banks' inflation targets. Only in countries where political shocks have caused the exchange rate to fall rapidly is inflation anywhere near target – and as Western central banks no longer explicitly target exchange rates, this rise in inflation had little to do with central banks. We now know that pouring money into banks and financial markets does not increase inflation when the transmission mechanisms by which money reaches the real economy are broken. When banks don't want to lend, and people don't want to borrow, inflation does not rise. The money created by QE went into asset markets instead, raising the prices of oil, commodities, property, bonds and stocks.

Had central banks given money to ordinary people so that they could spend or pay down their debts; had they given money to small businesses so that they could invest for the future; had they helped governments improve public infrastructure, build social housing and kick-start innovative technological developments; had they funded job creation programmes for the unemployed; in short, had central banks done QE for the People instead of QE for the Banks, the picture might now be very different. Inflation might now be closer to its target, growth might have returned, and – most importantly of all – people's incomes might have risen instead of stagnating for a decade.

So the most obvious rejoinder to those who fear that QE for the People would raise inflation is – yes, of course it would. That's the whole point. Bizarrely, central bankers whose policies have failed to raise inflation to target remain opposed to alternative policies that might succeed where theirs have failed. Their inflation forecasts have been wildly optimistic for the last decade, and yet they continue to produce forecasts that show inflation rising back to target 'soon', even though the policies of the last ten years have failed to achieve this and they have no plans to change the policies.

But, if central banks can't be trusted to do their jobs properly, for how long will central banks remain independent? If central bankers really value the independence of the institutions they serve, they should acknowledge the failure of their policies and be open to alternatives.

Box 4.1. Reversing QE for the People.

One of the arguments often advanced against QE for the People is that it would be difficult to reverse and that central banks would therefore be unable to control inflation. It is true that reversing some forms of QE for the People could be problematic. But there is emphatically no reason why this should result in a central bank losing control of inflation.

There are several different types of QE for the People. The approach to reversing it would differ depending on the type.

Buying the bonds of investment banks or sovereign wealth funds, or securities backed by bundles of SME loans, would be straightforward to reverse.

The central bank would simply sell or lend out the bonds, which would reduce the quantity of bank reserves and deposits in circulation and thus tighten monetary policy.

If the central bank had corporate bonds or equities on its balance sheet, these too could be sold. However, direct stakes in companies that are not actively traded, or for whose equity there is little private sector demand, could be difficult to offload. For this reason, it would be better for equity investments of this kind to be taken on by a public investment fund or bank rather than directly by the central bank. Bonds issued by that fund or bank would be likely to be much more easily sold at need.

Helicopter drops to individuals create a different problem. When the central bank buys assets from investors in a QE for the Banks programme, the assets sit on its balance sheet until either the central bank sells them or they expire. Currently, the Federal Reserve is not replacing assets that expire, so its balance sheet is shrinking. Similarly, if it sold assets, its balance sheet would shrink. When the central bank's balance sheet shrinks, so does the total quantity of base money in circulation. This is an automatic process.

However, for helicopter drops, no assets would be purchased. The balancing 'asset' for helicopter drops would look something like a perpetual loan. That couldn't itself be sold. But the central bank could offset it by issuing its own bonds to the private sector, either to financial markets or as savings products to the ordinary people to whom it had dropped money in the first place. People who bought those bonds would in effect be repaying the money that they had been given.

Another way of withdrawing a helicopter drop would be for the central bank to sell other assets on its balance sheet such as government bonds. But perhaps the most obvious way of reversing a helicopter drop to ordinary people would be to raise interest rates, since higher interest payments withdraw money from people's pockets.

Money financing of the government deficit could be reversed with tax rises. However, this dilutes the central bank's independent control of inflation. An alternative would be to raise interest rates, since interest payments drain money from the private sector in much the same way as taxes. Alternatively, the central bank could be given the power to raise (or lower) the rate of an indirect tax such as value-added tax (VAT).

Some (Weak) Objections to QE for the People

The sacred cow of central bank independence

The inflation fears discussed in Box 4.1 really amount to fear that the central bank will lose its independence. There is a deeply entrenched belief among economists and central bankers that inflation can only be kept under control if central banks are independent of government. In many jurisdictions, central bank independence is jealously guarded; in some, it is enshrined in law.

However, central bank independence is a fig leaf. The real need is for responsible government and strong institutions. Those who fear that helicopter money would cause runaway inflation believe that governments cannot be trusted to act responsibly, and that central banks cannot cooperate with government without losing control of inflation.

All forms of QE require cooperation between central bank and fiscal authority.[8] Unfortunately, opponents of QE for the People tend to confuse cooperation with captivity. If a central bank cooperates with a responsible government to drop enough money into the economy to ward off deflation after a major financial or economic shock, it has not compromised its independence. Cooperating with a fiscal authority is not the same as being captured by it.

Some (Weak) Objections to QE for the People

Since central banks have no direct relationship with ordinary people, they need government to help them distribute QE for the People. They could distribute it by, for example, creating accounts at the central bank for individuals, or sending people cheques. But they would need information held by government, such as social security numbers, to identify the people who should receive the money. In some countries, data protection rules would prohibit government from providing the central bank with this information. Government would need to communicate with the individuals concerned to advise them of their right to claim money from the central bank or to distribute cheques on behalf of the central bank. This form of cooperation would not diminish the central bank's independence or its control of inflation. The decision to do a helicopter drop would rest with the central bank, and the government would simply act as the agent of the central bank in the implementation of monetary policy.

If the government limited distribution of central bank money to certain groups only – for example, if the government decided that a helicopter drop should only go to those in receipt of certain state benefits – that would constitute some loss of independence for the central bank, since the central bank would not have control of money distribution.

Some (Weak) Objections to QE for the People

As the distribution of money influences inflation, there would be some impact on the central bank's ability to meet its inflation target. However, since the government would be restricting the distribution of money, it would tend to make the central bank's helicopter drop less inflationary, not more.

If the government also dictated to the central bank how much money to issue and when to issue it, the central bank would lose control of the drop. Would this result in runaway inflation? Well, it depends. Since the central bank would no longer have full control of base money creation, it would not be able to control inflation by itself. However, the combined government/central bank authority would still be able to control inflation if it could convince people that it was acting responsibly. The amount of new money distributed by the combined authority would probably raise inflation – after all, that would be its purpose. But in the past, combined fiscal and monetary authorities have successfully used helicopter drops to reflate economies without triggering hyperinflation. There is no reason to assume that they could not do so again.

There is also no reason to assume that a responsible government would necessarily dictate to a central bank how and when to do helicopter drops. A milder form of cooperation, where the central bank decides how much money to create and when to create it, but the fiscal authority determines its distribution, seems much more likely.

Fiscal dominance, where the government dictates monetary policy to the central bank, is a bigger risk when the central bank is supporting public investment projects. Political authorities could demand that the central bank guarantees bonds issued to finance public investment projects. Alternatively, they could require the central bank to buy the bonds and hold them to maturity. Either of these would effectively be money financing of longer-term public investment. Would this be compatible with the central bank's inflation-targeting mandate? Well, again, it would depend. If the proportion of such bonds on the central bank's balance sheet were small, and/or it had the freedom to issue its own bonds at need, then the central bank should be able to guarantee public investment bonds without losing control of inflation. But there is a risk that holding these bonds, or routinely intervening in the market to keep their yields low, could impede the central bank's ability to manage interest rates.

Central banks use interest rates to dampen economic fluctuations, both on the downside and the upside. Interest rates are a blunt instrument, and they are only partially effective because of the 'lower bound' problem – the fact that once interest rates are below zero, people find ways of avoiding what is essentially a tax on deposits. Nonetheless, they are an essential weapon in the central bank's armoury.

Public investment bonds initially sold to the private sector would have market interest rates. If they were guaranteed by the central bank, the rates would be the risk-free rate plus a term premium. Even without a central bank guarantee, the rates would be similar if investors believed that the central bank would always buy the bonds if the yields started to rise. However, if the central bank's primary mandate were to control inflation, it could not guarantee to buy the bonds. The central bank's job is to manage interest rates in general, not to control the yields on specific types of bonds. Even if the yields on investment bonds headed for the moon, an inflation-targeting central bank could not buy them unless it were necessary to meet its inflation target. If it needed to raise interest rates, it might even sell its existing holdings.

If an inflation-targeting central bank financed investment projects that commenced during a downturn when rates were very low, it could find itself under political pressure to guarantee that those rates would stay low for the duration of the project, even though interest rates would rise as the economy recovered. Which would win – the imperative to keep rates low on public investment bonds, or the central bank's price stability mandate?

The biggest risk of all arises from explicit central bank financing of the government deficit. Hyperinflation is indeed a risk when a captive central bank prints money at will on the orders of a profligate and corrupt government. Those who oppose QE for the People point to Weimar, Zimbabwe and, now, Venezuela as awful warnings of what happens when central banks are captive to profligate governments.

But why should we assume that governments will always be profligate? A few are, of course. But since the financial crisis, many Western governments have been thrifty to the point of miserliness. If anything, it is central banks that have been profligate, not governments.

Central bank financing of even quite a large government deficit (or direct central bank payments to ordinary citizens, which amounts to the same thing) is a much better way of reflating an economy than piles of asset purchases on secondary markets. In his book 'Debt and the Devil', Adair Turner says that when interest rates are on the floor and both the private and the public sector are highly indebted, normal fiscal and monetary policy are impotent.[9] Central bank financing of public spending, one way or another, is the only game in town.

Central bank independence has become something of a sacred cow, and sacred cows have a distressing tendency to impede rational behaviour. In a deflationary slump, the primary need is to get money flowing round the economy. When normal monetary transmission mechanisms are broken, extraordinary measures are needed. Irrational fears cannot be allowed to prevent central banks and governments around the world from cooperating to restore their economies. The last ten years have shown us that when fear of debt and inflation prevents central banks and fiscal authorities from making effective use of the central bank's money creation powers, the real risk is a long-lasting deflationary slump.

The myth of central bank insolvency

Mark Carney, Governor of the Bank of England, bluntly dismissed helicopter money because of its effect on the central bank's balance sheet. 'I am not a believer in the concept of helicopter money', he said in testimony to the UK's House of Lords.[10] And he went on:

In effect, what is being asked is that a central bank cancels the debt that is purchased from the Government ... In doing so, the bank puts a hole in its bank sheet and moves into negative equity. In order for that stimulus to be there in perpetuity, it has to hold negative equity forever. In other words, Government never has to recapitalize the central bank ... We would also create a fundamental problem with the outstanding reserves in the banking system. ... on which we must pay interest. That is not a problem when rates are low ... but would become one when you started to take away the stimulus, the economy recovered and the policy actually succeeded. We would not have an asset on the other side to meet that liability, and so we would end up in a compounding ponzi scheme. There is no way of structuring round that.

Carney assumes firstly, that QE for the People would explicitly finance a government deficit, and secondly, that it would cause an increase in interest-bearing bank reserves. Neither of these would necessarily be the case. But his criticism is nevertheless significant. He is in effect saying that QE for the People could result in the permanent insolvency of the central bank.

The risk is that people could lose confidence in a central bank that was permanently insolvent, which could encourage people to use alternatives to government money, or even trigger hyperinflation. How likely is it that people would be so concerned about negative equity on a central bank balance sheet that they lost all confidence in its liabilities? Well, it all depends on how the central bank is viewed by the public. For helicopter drops to be trusted even if they caused the technical insolvency of the central bank, people would need to believe that the central bank's decision to drop helicopter money was justified by expected future returns. Those future returns would be higher GDP, higher interest rates and improving living standards. The hope of future prosperity is a great motivator.

From an accounting perspective, Carney's comments about 'negative equity' are misleading. Helicopter money can't put a 'hole' in a central bank's balance sheet. The rules of accounting dictate that when new liabilities are created, equivalent assets must simultaneously be either purchased or created. Helicopter money would not involve asset purchase, so a new asset to the value of the drop must be created. What would this asset be?

If the central bank were financing a government deficit (or writing off government debt), as Carney envisages, the asset would be a perpetual loan to the government. Since this loan could bear interest,

Carney's claim that helicopter money would result in compounding insolvency because of interest payments on reserves is wrong. Provided the interest the central bank received on its loan covered the interest it paid on reserves, there would be no Ponzi, at least at the central bank. The interest on the loan would simply be a claim on future tax receipts.

If the central bank were doing a helicopter drop directly to households, the asset would be a zero-interest perpetual loan to the private sector. In this case, paying interest on reserves could theoretically become a compounding Ponzi as interest rates rose. But any asset held on the central bank's balance sheet can bear a lower interest rate than that on reserves. For example, central banks carry lots of gold on their balance sheets. Gold bears no interest. Does that mean that paying interest on reserves is a Ponzi scheme?

Insolvency is a factor of the whole balance sheet, not one part of it. It is entirely possible for part of the central bank's asset base to return less than the interest the central bank pays on reserves, if other assets return more than the interest on reserves. These days, central banks have on their balance sheets assets that return far more than the interest paid on reserves. Although these assets carry credit and market risk which could mean that their returns drop below zero, it is hard to see that helicopter drops would seriously disrupt the solvency of a central bank with a widely diversified asset portfolio.

But even if they did, the central bank is not alone. As Ricardo Reis observed, 'Insofar as its liabilities are supported by the fiscal authorities, the central bank cannot be insolvent separately from the solvency of the overall government.'[11] How likely is it that a central bank would be so completely cut off from government that it had no guarantee of solvency?

If the government guaranteed to cover any difference between the interest payments the central bank made on reserves and the returns on its assets, helicopter money would present no risk to the central bank's solvency. In fact, governments have already had to provide such a guarantee for conventional QE programmes.[12] The UK government even set up a special purpose vehicle to hold the assets, thus safeguarding the Bank of England's own balance sheet. There could be a similar arrangement for helicopter money.

The loan either to the government or the private sector would have to persist forever but, provided the central bank had a credible guarantee of fiscal support, this would not matter. The prospect of the central bank carrying a perpetual irredeemable loan on its balance sheet, even at zero interest, should not be a barrier to helicopter money. However, if the government could not be trusted to back its central bank, a shortage of tradable assets on the central bank's balance sheet could render it unable to guarantee the value of money. In this, Carney is correct. Hyperinflation is indeed a risk if the government won't or can't back its central bank. QE for the People requires responsible government.

People wouldn't spend the money

At the opposite extreme from those who argue that helicopter money would be wildly inflationary because people would spend the money as fast as they got it, are those who argue that helicopter drops wouldn't stimulate the economy because people wouldn't spend the money.

There are several variants of this argument. Firstly, people might simply refuse to use the money because they don't regard it as 'theirs'. Richard Koo, for example, says Japanese households would not spend bills dropped from the sky in a Friedman-style helicopter distribution, they would turn them in to the police. 'A helicopter money policy can only work if the people in a country have little sense of right and wrong', he says.[13]

Koo also says that shops and businesses might not accept physical currency distributed by means of a helicopter drop. This seems odd: one $100 dollar bill looks much like another, after all. His argument appears to be that dropping money to households to counteract the effects of falling bank lending would destroy trust in the currency. Shopkeepers and businesses might reject helicopter money if the distribution took the form of specially issued notes, bonds or coins, perhaps with a timestamp to ensure they were spent. But this surely depends on the credibility of the institutions involved. Shopkeepers and businesses will accept specially issued notes, bonds or coins if they trust that banks will exchange them for real money at par. In turn, banks will exchange specially issued notes, bonds or coins at par if they trust the central bank to make good their reserve loss.

In any case, today's helicopters are electronic. Would households reject money paid into their own deposit accounts by the central bank? It seems unlikely. Would shopkeepers reject electronically delivered helicopter money presented to them by households as payment for goods? It is hard to see how they could. One digital dollar is indistinguishable from another. What is paid out of my bank account, or my wallet, may be my wages, my savings, money I have borrowed from the bank (my overdraft), money given to me by the government (e.g. welfare benefits, pension), or money given to me by the central bank. Shopkeepers have no means of distinguishing between money from any of these sources. So, a shopkeeper who didn't want to accept helicopter money would have to refuse to accept any electronic money at all. They would only do this if they thought electronic money was worthless. We are back to our old friend hyperinflation again.

Another argument is that helicopter drops would not work because people would save the money instead of spending it. Rich people no doubt would do exactly this, since they wouldn't need additional spending money. People saving for their retirements might stash the money away too. They might put the money into interest-bearing savings accounts and leave it there. They might buy investments such as stocks, bonds, gold, art or property. Or they might even store it under the bed.

If everyone saved the money, the economic boost from helicopter money would be similar to that from QE for the Banks – not zero, but disappointing. To improve the economic boost, money could be distributed in ways that discouraged saving – for example, by issuing prepaid cash cards that expired after say six months and could not be exchanged for cash. Alternatively, helicopter drops could be targeted at poorer people, who would be more likely to spend the money. For example, government could decide that helicopter money should only go to people in receipt of certain state benefits, or should not go to people who pay higher rate taxes. Provided those who were eligible for targeted helicopter money were a large enough proportion of the population, targeted drops could give a significant economic boost at lower cost than indiscriminate drops. They also might be more attractive politically, since giving government money to the rich is seldom a vote-winner.

However, evidence suggests that most people would either spend the money or use it to pay down debt. Helicopter money would still work if people used it to pay down debt. Freeing people of debt would give people more money for non-essential things such as clothes, meals out, holidays and furnishings. They might also borrow to invest in, for example, improving their home or their skills. As private debt reduced, therefore, spending would increase, creating work for businesses and generating jobs and wage growth, which ultimately is the goal of helicopter money. A survey conducted in 2012 reported that forty per cent of Australians spent the cash windfalls given them by their government in the Great Recession of 2008–2009. A further thirty-five per cent used them to pay debts.[14] Only a quarter of Australians said they saved or invested the money. Thus, the total proportion of Australians who spent the money in ways that directly boosted the economy could be as high as seventy-five per cent. This could be a useful rule of thumb for estimating the proportion of a helicopter drop that would be spent productively.

Another argument against helicopter money is what economists call 'Ricardian equivalence'. If the helicopter drop increased the government's deficit, people would save the money instead of spending it, because they would expect to have to pay it back later in the form of higher taxes. The Australian survey found that people who were worried about the size of government debt were significantly more likely to save the money than people who were not worried. But even among those who were worried about government debt, over half spent the money anyway. It seems that the benefits from money now tend to override worries about the tax costs later.

The final argument in this section is that governments might use central bank support as an opportunity to enact severe fiscal cutbacks, which is equivalent to the government saving the money provided by the central bank. If it did, then the central bank money would still have some stimulatory effect on the economy, but the offsetting fiscal tightening would redistribute money from the poor to the rich, making it less effective.

Willem Buiter argues that if it is done properly, helicopter money will always work, regardless of what people do with the money.[15]

Buiter says that QE for the People will always boost aggregate demand (i.e. get people spending) if the following three conditions hold:

- Since base money doesn't normally bear interest (though at present bank reserves do carry a positive interest rate in some countries), there must be benefits from holding base money other than its pecuniary rate of return.
- Base money is irredeemable – viewed as an asset by the holder but not as a liability by the issuer.
- The price of money is positive (the interest rate doesn't drop below zero).

The first condition is satisfied when people (and banks) hold base money even though they have interest-bearing alternatives. Base money consists of physical currency and bank reserves. Most people use physical currency to make small purchases, and banks always use reserves to make electronic payments, whether on their own account or on behalf of their customers. So, people keep cash in their wallets, and banks hold reserves.

The second condition has been satisfied in most countries since the gold standard came to an end in 1971. Base money is not convertible to gold or any other commodity. The 'promise to pay' on the face of a Bank of England note means nothing but a promise to pay more of itself. So, if you take a £10 note to the Bank of England and ask for it to be redeemed, they will give you another £10 note, or perhaps ten £1 coins.[16] Money that is not backed by anything except the promise of its issuer is known as 'fiat' money. Currently, almost all government-issued money is fiat money. Because it does not expire and is not redeemable in anything but itself, fiat base money is not really 'debt'. It is more like a share in the current and future wealth of the country.

The third condition is usually met, even in a recession. Central banks cut interest rates nearly to zero in 2008, and some have since experimented with slightly negative interest rates. But the fact that physical cash doesn't bear interest is an obstacle to negative rates. If central banks cut interest rates more than a few basis points below zero, people will stuff banknotes into mattresses instead of putting money into interest-bearing bank accounts, and banks will fill their vaults with cash instead of holding more electronic reserves than they immediately need for payments. So the price of money generally remains positive.

There is a further condition too. For QE for the People to work, the increase in the monetary base must be permanent. The central bank and government must give no hint whatsoever that the money might ever be clawed back through higher taxes or interest rates. As the economist Paul Krugman puts it, the central bank must credibly commit to being 'irresponsible'.[17] This is quite a challenge for an inflation-targeting central bank whose policymakers grew up in the inflationary 1970s. But if central bankers can overcome their fears and allow QE for the People to do its job, then it will always work.

Why would QE for the People always work? Buiter says that, provided there is a real-world use for base money and its supply is not eroded by negative interest rates, expansion of base money forces the government to increase spending one way or another. Conventional QE has this effect too, but the problem is that when monetary policy transmission mechanisms are blocked, the new base money churns around on financial markets pumping up asset prices, rather than stimulating spending and investment in the real economy. QE for the People would direct money to households and businesses which could spend it productively.

We have wasted ten years trying to make QE for the Banks work while pursuing fiscal policies that render it ineffective. Scared governments have preferred to impose misery on their populations rather than cooperate with their central banks to implement policies that would quickly restore jobs and living standards.

QE for the People isn't needed

This is perhaps the most significant objection to QE for the People. The argument is that the only reason sovereign governments can't restore growth and raise living standards is that financial markets and/or supranational authorities such as the IMF impose arbitrary and unfair borrowing and spending limits. Rather than using central bank financing to circumvent these limits, governments should take back control of their own finances.

For helicopter drops, there is a simple answer. There is a clear distinction between fiscal policy and helicopter money. The purpose of fiscal policy is to redistribute existing resources. The purpose of helicopter money is to create and distribute new money. Increasing the base money stock to counter deflation caused by falling bank lending is the central bank's job.

Governments can do one-off money distributions without involving the central bank. But, as these would be financed by current borrowing and future taxation, they would not cause an increase in the money supply. If the goal is to counteract falling bank lending by increasing the amount of base money in circulation, the central bank must be involved. Even if helicopter money is physically distributed by the government, and the central bank finances the government deficit arising from that distribution, it is still the central bank that creates the money.

Helicopter drops should be a normal part of an independent central bank's armoury. It is ridiculous to say that distributing money to financial markets is monetary policy, and therefore the central bank's responsibility, but distributing money to ordinary people is fiscal policy and therefore the government's responsibility. Money is money, and the central bank is responsible for it.

Some (Weak) Objections to QE for the People

Even in the Eurozone, money creation is the central bank's responsibility. The ECB can and should do helicopter drops to all EU citizens regardless of nationality.[18] As the payments would be made directly to people, not to governments, and would be for the same amount irrespective of average wages or tax and welfare arrangements in Eurozone countries, they would not fall foul of Article 123 of the Lisbon Treaty, which prohibits central banks in EU countries from financing their own governments directly.[19] It could perhaps be argued that the ECB's helicopter drops would increase tax revenue and therefore constitute monetary financing of government, but the obvious counter would be for ECB helicopter drops to be ineligible for taxation.

If we value central bank independence at all, we should counter the weasel words that would restrict the central bank's domain and hence its effectiveness. Money that goes to ordinary people is far more effective at restoring growth and raising inflation than money that only goes to financial markets. The central bank needs to be able to distribute money as widely as possible, not have its scope artificially restricted.

True helicopter drops are only possible if the central bank is involved. For public investment, however, the argument that the government can and should do whatever is needed without direct central bank involvement is much more powerful. As the Bank of England's chief economist, Andy Haldane, explains, the central bank's job is to manage cyclical variation in the economy, not to determine its long-term direction:

> When it comes to those structural features of the economy, central banks do not have the tools to affect lasting change. Central bank tools are cyclical, rather than structural, because their impact on the economy is temporary, not permanent. We do not build schools, colleges, houses, roads, railways or banks. Nor do we finance them. Those tools, rightly, are in the hands either of governments or private companies. So too is the financing of them.[20]

Those who want the central bank to finance public investment need to ask themselves to what extent this distinction between cyclical and structural should be blurred. If government comes to rely on its central bank to finance public spending programmes, there is a risk that the central bank will not be able to deal with short-term economic fluctuations effectively.

That said, the distortions in asset markets caused by central bank QE have made structural changes to many economies that may prove to be permanent. The boundary between government and central bank is already very blurred. Arguably, too, such a distinction is specious. IMF research shows that deep economic recessions cause permanent structural changes to the economy.[21] In view of this, does it really matter whether the investment needed to pull the economy out of its slump is financed by public borrowing or the central bank? If government is constrained in its ability to borrow, the central bank can and should step in to prevent lasting damage. Some argue that the central bank should step in anyway, since there is a long-term cost to public borrowing. But what if there is no limit to government borrowing and the 'long-term cost' is simply a fiscal transfer between different social groups? Should the central bank still step in?

This is not as unlikely as it sounds. For global reserve currency issuers such as the US and the UK, the fear of government default is overblown. For much of the last two centuries the UK's public debt stock (in relation to GDP) was far higher than it is today, yet the UK never defaulted on its debt. Furthermore, innovative types of government bond such as GDP-linked bonds can make it possible for governments to borrow far more without debt service becoming unsustainable.[22]

Research by Paul Barratt of the IMF showed that there is effectively no limit to borrowing for a reserve currency issuer such as the US or UK as long as the interest rate on its public debt is below its growth rate.[23] And at the UK's National Institute for Economic and Social Research (NIESR), Roger Farmer and Pavel Zabczyk showed that rising debt puts downwards pressure on interest rates, making the costs of even very large amounts of debt affordable.[24]

The idea that government debt is a burden for future generations is also a myth. Government debt is the savings of the private sector. When it is mostly held by the citizens of its own country, the interest payments are tax credits for those citizens. Since those with the most savings tend to be the old and the rich, this can raise inequality, but that can be offset by fiscal transfers in the opposite direction. Conversely, since investment drives productivity, which in turn determines wages and living standards, failure to invest can materially impoverish future generations.

The public debt of the world's major reserve currency issuers is always in demand, even in a slump. Restricting its supply significantly depresses interest rates, which is particularly hard on older people who are living on the returns from savings. It can also interfere with the smooth operation of financial markets, with unfortunate consequences for private sector investment.

When a government can borrow freely at very low interest rates, it is hard to see any economic justification for the central bank financing public investment projects. Indeed, issuing more government debt rather than relying on central bank money to finance public investment could improve the operation of financial markets and relieve hard-pressed savers. Government debt is widely used as collateral for short-term borrowing and as a safe home for retirement savings. When there is an insufficient supply of government debt to meet demand, interest rates fall and financial markets become stressed. The same objections arise regarding central bank financing of job creation programmes and other welfare spending. If the governments of the world's reserve currency issuers want to put their unemployed to work or give money to the poor, they can do so simply by increasing government deficits. There is little justification for central bank financing of government borrowing while interest rates are on the floor.

Governments of most developed countries can undertake large-scale public investment programmes financed with bonds issued by public investment banks, sovereign wealth funds or (if local law allows) simply by the government itself. Their central banks could buy those bonds as part of day-to-day monetary operations, or – in the event of another economic downturn – as part of a 'conventional' QE programme. There is no need for explicit monetary financing of public investment.

However, not all governments can borrow whatever they need. Since no central bank can issue unlimited quantities of another country's currency, governments of countries that use currencies they don't issue can't borrow without limit. This applies to many developing countries where the US dollar or the euro is needed to pay for investment and imports. For them, central bank financing (in local currency) of government spending (in a foreign currency) carries significant risk of hyperinflation. Any attempt to use the central bank to fund government deficits would be likely to cause bond yields to spike. Helicopter money might still be possible without triggering a run on the currency, though, if it could be credibly seen as both distinct from government spending and strictly short term.

Some governments in the Eurozone also can't borrow any more. Although the Eurozone as a whole is a reserve currency issuer with its own central bank, its member states are not. They don't issue their own currencies, and their central banks are part of the Eurosystem of central banks that is led by the ECB. Their governments must finance themselves by borrowing, and they cannot rely on the ECB backstopping their bonds: 'Outright Monetary Transactions' (OMT), the ECB's guarantee programme for the bonds of Eurozone member states, is so heavily conditioned on fiscal austerity that it has never been used.[25] But many Eurozone countries desperately need investment. Could a Eurozone-wide public investment programme financed by the ECB be a way forward?

The short answer is no. In the Eurozone, the prohibition on central bank financing of governments is extremely strict. It would be difficult for the ECB to buy public investment bonds issued by governments, even on the open market. The ECB can buy bonds issued by the European Investment Bank (EIB). "'Juncker's Plan' aims to kick-start investment all over the European Union (not just the Eurozone) with a combination of private and EIB finance, implicitly backed by the ECB.[26] However, creative though Juncker's Plan is, it doesn't go nearly far enough. In the absence of a fully integrated financial system, Eurozone-wide automatic stabilizers,[27] and fiscal transfers from richer to poorer states, the ECB's monetary policy is inevitably too loose for stronger states and too tight for weaker ones. Furthermore, the ECB has increasingly taken on quasi-governmental responsibilities, notably in the treatment of weaker Eurozone states; for example, it participated in the 'Troika' that oversaw Greece's bailout programme. The budget discipline necessarily imposed on weaker states because they lack both central bank support and fiscal transfers makes it impossible for weaker states to put enough money into their economies to restore growth and reduce unemployment. Six years after the Eurozone crisis, unemployment remains in double digits in much of the Eurozone, and in some countries it is still over twenty per cent at the time of writing. If this situation continues, at some point there will be a political reckoning.

Since 2015, the ECB has made matters even worse by effectively subsidizing the governments of stronger states in the monetary union while giving little support to the weakest ones. The principal beneficiary of ECB QE is Germany, which at the time of writing can finance itself at negative rates for about ten years to come. Growth has returned in the Eurozone mainly because of very large current account surpluses in stronger Northern countries, largely due to a combination of tight fiscal policy with QE. In effect, the stronger countries in the

Eurozone are exporting the ECB's QE in order to buy aggregate demand from the rest of the world. This is not a sustainable policy: the US is already indicating that it is unwilling to play consumer of last resort to the Eurozone at the expense of its own producers.

It is imperative that the Eurozone changes direction. The ECB must stop subsidizing the governments of stronger states and embark on helicopter drops to all Eurozone citizens. Surplus countries need to relax their tight fiscal stance, and deficit countries need to be supported to reflate their economies with targeted fiscal and monetary stimulus. To do this, Eurozone governments will need to cooperate more closely both with each other and with the ECB. Article 123 needs to be replaced with a new law that encourages such cooperation, and the ECB needs to have unemployment added to its mandate. And the Stability and Growth Pact, that encourages strong states to build up surpluses while preventing governments of weaker countries from reflating their economies, needs to be torn up. If this does not happen, I fear the Eurozone is doomed.

5

Lessons for the Next Depression

The democratic challenge

QE for the People requires close cooperation between central bank and government. But at present there is an antagonistic relationship between some central banks and their governments. This is rooted in fear of government, and indeed of democracy. It is no surprise that some mainstream economists who support QE for the People want deficit and debt monetization to be done at arms' length from the elected government, perhaps by means of an unelected 'fiscal council'. The reason often advanced is that QE for the People must not be dependent on the whims of politicians whose primary interest is in getting re-elected. This sounds reasonable, but it is enormously dangerous.

QE for the Banks had little democratic legitimacy, particularly in the EU. It was widely seen as a policy conducted by central banks to benefit bankers. This isn't true, but that doesn't matter. What matters is that many people believe it. The rise of populist politicians is in part driven by anger that remote, unelected bureaucrats are making decisions that affect the lives of ordinary people. The 'Take Back Control' slogan in the UK's EU referendum spoke to those who felt that decisions were being made in which they had no say. It is no accident that their anger was aimed at the European Union: nowhere is the democratic deficit in monetary policy more evident than in the Eurozone, where the ECB can force elected governments to abandon policies they have been democratically mandated to deliver.

QE for the People must not make the same mistake. If it is to have any credibility, it must not only deliver money to the people, it must be accountable to them too. It cannot be used as an excuse to water down still further the democratic legitimacy of government and institutions. Central banks must be clearly accountable to the people they serve, perhaps through direct election of central bank governors and committees, or at least, enabling elected representatives of the people to set central bank mandates and hold technocrats to account.

Antagonism between governments and central banks must end. Governments are not naughty children to be 'disciplined' by central banks, and central bankers are not high priests who alone can placate the angry economic gods. The sacred cow of central bank independence must be slaughtered. There needs to be a new era of cooperation between governments and central banks, and a recognition by both that they are not infallible.

The fear of inflation must also end. Runaway inflation is terrible, but so too are debt deflation and poverty. When the economy is in a slump, fear of inflation cannot be allowed to prevent central banks and governments cooperating to restore prosperity.

And finally, there must be zero tolerance of policies that exacerbate inequality and hurt the poor. Pumping up asset prices for the rich while cutting back social safety nets for the poor does not restore prosperity. All it does is make ordinary people angry. After ten years of this, it is only surprising that there are not mobs with pitchforks hammering at the gates of governments across the Western world.

In some European countries, unemployment is far too high and growth far too low. The ECB can and should do helicopter drops to all Eurozone citizens. And the EU can and should support large-scale investment programmes targeted at poorer countries, to reduce unemployment, raise living standards and attract businesses. These programmes can be funded by the European Investment Bank and backed by the ECB in a QE for the People bond-purchase programme.

In other Western countries, the current problem is not high unemployment, but productivity stagnation, largely caused by the collapse of both private and public investment. QE for the People could support a large increase in public investment, but this would be a fig-leaf over the real problem, which is the fear of government debt and deficits whipped up by small-state ideologues.

Now is the time to put in place the central bank–government cooperation that will be needed when the next economic downturn hits. If there isn't a public investment bank or sovereign wealth fund, create one. There is no need to instruct the central bank to buy its bonds: it can issue them to the private sector to fund much-needed investment in these countries. The central bank will stand ready to buy those bonds, and more, when the need arises.

Additionally, we need to end legal or operational restrictions that prevent the central bank cooperating effectively with the government. Allow the government to run an overdraft with the central bank for day-to-day spending. Consider giving some tax powers to the central bank, such as control of VAT. Perhaps create a democratically elected fiscal council, or give enhanced powers to the debt management office, so that the central bank's money creation powers can be closely coupled with the government's ability to create safe assets to meet the population's long-term savings needs.

To silence those who shout about central bank insolvency and hyperinflation whenever anyone suggests helicopter money, we need to write into law permanent fiscal backing for the central bank. Even better, we need to stop accounting for the government and the central bank separately. Produce full consolidated accounts, as a corporation would.

Could QE for the People democratize the creation of money?

Throughout this book, I have assumed that QE for the People, like QE for the Banks, would be a short-term stimulus to pull the economy out of a slump. But Milton Friedman said that central bank financing of small government deficits should be the normal way of putting money into an economy.[1] This raises the intriguing possibility of reinventing the role of the central bank and the function of money creation in the economy. What if, instead of merely being an ad-hoc stimulus at the combined discretion of the central bank and government, QE for the People became the principal means of managing the economy?

This is in effect what advocates of 'sovereign money' and full reserve banking schemes propose. All money in the economy would be created by the central bank and spent directly into the economy through a permanent form of QE for the People. Money would no longer be backed by private sector debt, but by the future productive potential of the economy.

It is beyond the scope of this book to discuss the merits and demerits of such schemes. But one of the benefits of QE for the People could be to democratize the creation and distribution of money. Perhaps, if used permanently, QE for the People could return power to the people?

Looking to the future

QE for the People could also help the world address three major challenges that threaten human life as we know it: the problem of ageing, the changing nature of work, and climate change.

Lessons for the Next Depression

The problem of ageing

Populations are ageing rapidly across the entire developed world, and much of the developing world too. Persistently low birth rates in many countries, coupled with rising longevity due to improvements in healthcare and nutrition, is increasing the proportion of elderly to working-age people. In some countries, this is exacerbated by emigration of the young.

As a result, government spending on the elderly is projected to rise considerably. Germany, for example, is projected to spend 12.5 per cent of GDP on pensions by 2050.[2] Elderly people also make high demands on health and social care services: as the proportion of elderly in the population grows, the cost of these services for working-age adults will inevitably rise. The picture is one of a growing tax burden on a shrinking workforce.

To relieve the pressure on stretched fiscal finances, people are being encouraged to work for longer and save more. Most countries are raising statutory retirement ages, though this is extremely unpopular. Some countries are also introducing coercive savings schemes – for example, the UK's 'auto-enrolment' forces all employees to save for a pension.

But persistently higher saving results in persistently lower demand which is resistant to monetary policy. Forced saving encumbers part of people's incomes. If wages do not rise to accommodate the higher saving – and real wages have been stagnant for some years now in most Western countries – then people must either cut back spending or take on additional debt. Older people find it more difficult to borrow than younger ones, and may be reluctant to do so anyway, since they have less time to repay the debt. A central bank whose sole approach to monetary policy is to encourage borrowing will struggle to get either inflation or growth off the floor when the government is introducing forced saving policies and/or the ageing population has a strong saving habit.

An ageing workforce also causes structural changes in the economy. Older people's skills can become obsolete due to technological change. Older people are also more likely to work part time, to eschew work that takes them away from home, and to have health problems or caring responsibilities that restrict the types of work they can undertake. As the proportion of older people in the economy grows, therefore, we might expect poorer productivity, which, if not addressed, would result in persistently lower GDP growth. Governments need

Table 5.1. Demographic old-age dependency ratios:
Historical and projected values, 1950–2075.

	1950	1975	2000	2015	2025	2050	2075
OECD members							
Australia	14.0	16.0	20.6	25.0	31.2	41.2	48.4
Austria	17.3	27.1	24.9	30.5	37.1	59.4	63.1
Belgium	18.1	25.2	28.3	30.6	37.1	51.0	54.0
Canada	14.0	15.4	20.5	26.1	36.2	48.1	54.5
Chile	8.6	11.3	13.1	17.0	23.6	43.0	61.2
Czech Republic	13.9	22.7	21.9	28.8	37.1	58.9	55.6
Denmark	15.6	23.7	24.2	33.0	37.7	45.3	53.4
Estonia	19.3	21.2	25.0	31.0	39.2	56.3	59.0
Finland	11.9	18.1	24.8	35.0	44.0	48.8	54.7
France	19.5	24.5	27.3	33.3	40.9	52.3	55.8
Germany	16.2	26.5	26.5	34.8	41.4	59.2	63.1
Greece	12.4	20.9	26.7	33.0	39.2	73.4	75.2
Hungary	13.2	21.3	24.5	27.9	36.6	52.4	57.6
Iceland	14.1	18.1	20.2	23.1	31.5	45.7	58.4
Ireland	20.9	21.4	18.0	22.3	29.0	49.9	50.9
Israel	7.1	15.2	18.8	21.1	25.2	32.1	39.4
Italy	14.3	21.6	29.2	37.8	45.6	72.4	67.0
Japan	9.9	12.7	27.3	46.2	54.4	77.8	75.3
Korea	6.3	8.2	11.2	19.4	31.7	72.4	78.8
Latvia	18.1	21.9	25.1	31.5	39.0	52.3	52.0
Luxembourg	15.8	22.6	22.9	22.0	26.4	42.0	47.1
Mexico	7.9	9.6	10.0	11.4	14.8	32.2	53.7
Netherlands	13.9	19.3	21.9	30.2	39.0	53.0	59.7
New Zealand	16.3	16.9	20.3	25.1	32.5	43.6	54.5
Norway	16.0	24.9	25.9	27.4	32.5	43.1	51.2
Poland	9.4	17.1	20.1	24.3	36.4	60.8	73.3
Portugal	13.0	19.6	26.8	34.6	42.4	73.2	77.6
Slovak Republic	11.9	18.3	18.6	21.5	31.4	53.9	58.0
Slovenia	12.5	19.0	22.4	28.8	41.1	66.8	60.2
Spain	12.8	19.0	26.9	30.6	38.6	77.5	70.4
Sweden	16.8	26.3	29.5	33.8	38.2	45.5	51.6
Switzerland	15.8	21.5	24.9	29.0	35.4	54.6	58.1
Turkey	6.5	10.0	11.4	13.4	17.3	36.2	54.8

Table 5.1 (*cont.*)

	1950	1975	2000	2015	2025	2050	2075
United Kingdom	17.9	25.5	27.0	31.0	35.9	48.0	53.0
United States	14.2	19.7	20.9	24.6	32.9	40.3	49.3
OECD	**13.9**	**19.5**	**22.5**	**27.9**	**35.2**	**53.2**	**58.6**
Argentina	7.5	14.1	18.6	19.5	21.8	31.8	44.6
Brazil	6.5	8.0	9.3	13.0	18.3	40.1	62.3
China	8.5	8.8	11.4	14.5	22.3	47.9	58.8
India	6.4	7.6	8.7	10.0	12.7	22.0	37.0
Indonesia	8.6	7.9	8.7	8.7	11.6	23.1	32.5
Russian Federation	8.7	15.5	20.4	20.7	30.1	40.0	37.6
Saudi Arabia	7.5	7.6	6.1	4.8	7.5	27.4	40.6
South Africa	8.5	8.1	7.8	9.0	11.1	17.8	29.0
EU28	14.7	21.2	24.3	29.9	37.5	55.9	59.7

Note: This ratio is defined as the number of individuals aged 65 and over per 100 people of working age (between 20 and 64).
Source: United Nations World Population prospects, 2017 revision: From the OECD's *Pensions at a Glance,* 2017 edition.

to invest in technology that raises productivity, particularly among those who have physical and mental limitations, and encourage lifelong learning to keep skills current.

Japan's government debt/GDP is by far the highest in the world. However, ever since the Bank of Japan started buying Japanese government bonds as part of its QE programme, the debt/GDP measure has become less and less realistic. At the time of writing the Bank of Japan owns over forty per cent of Japanese government bonds and is buying up bonds faster than the government can issue them. Officially, these are temporary purchases. But the sheer scale of the Bank of Japan's purchases, and the fact that they have been wholly ineffective at raising inflation, means the bonds may never be sold back to the private sector. In effect, the Bank of Japan is financing the Japanese government's fiscal deficit, enabling the government to increase spending substantially without fear of debt default. This is, of course, QE for the People.

Inevitably, the Bank of Japan is being criticized for financing the government deficit. There are dark warnings of hyperinflation, notably – just as in 1932 – from Americans.[3] But hyperinflation occurs when the population rejects the currency, and Japan's demographics make this highly unlikely. The population already has a median age of 44 and rising, and Japanese savings are almost entirely in yen and yen-denominated assets. Why on earth would people approaching the end of their working lives reject the currency in which the savings they will need in retirement are denominated?

Accommodating the savings need of an ageing population requires a government to run either a fiscal deficit or a large trade surplus. Low domestic demand – characteristic of an ageing population – does tend to result in trade surpluses, because there is little import pressure. If only a few countries were experiencing rapid population ageing, and the rest had young and growing populations, then for those countries to pursue policies aimed at maintaining a high saving ratio and a large current account surplus would make sense. But when most of the countries in the world are ageing rapidly, policies that rely on importing demand from other countries are beggar-my-neighbour policies.

Fortunately, there is an alternative. QE for the People could be deployed to finance government deficit spending to maintain the living standards of all those retirees, thus supporting domestic demand, while QE for the Banks could be deployed to support the value of the assets they hold as retirement savings. This is what the government of the country with the oldest population is currently doing. The Japanese central bank is buying up yen-denominated assets and financing a large programme of deficit spending by the Japanese government. There is no sign of hyperinflation – indeed, even with all this fiscal and monetary stimulus, inflation and interest rates remain on the floor. Clearly, monetizing government deficits when there is a chronic demand shortfall due to an ageing population doesn't cause runaway inflation.

It is time to break the monetization taboo.[4] In an ageing world, stagnation and deflation due to low aggregate demand are the main risks. Helicopter money and central bank financing of fiscal deficits are the most powerful ways of raising domestic demand. Central banks and governments should not hesitate to use them.[5] In the sunset of a civilization, debt monetization is a friend.[6]

The threat of automation

In 2011, in a groundbreaking report, the UK's Work Foundation postulated that automation is eliminating routine semi-skilled jobs and forcing people into lower-skill, lower-paid jobs:

> Since the early 1990s sustained growth in high wage, analytical, non-routine jobs; an expansion of manual, lower wage jobs; and a contraction of routine, middle wage jobs has led to a 'hollowing out' of the labour market in developed economies. This creates an hourglass-shaped labour market.[7]

Manufacturing is becoming the province of robots. So too are routine skilled service jobs, particularly clerical and administration roles. Highly skilled humans control the robots, and other humans are relegated to low-paid, low-skilled service roles, particularly those involving face-to-face interaction with other humans. The secure, well-paid jobs of the past – many of them in manufacturing – are disappearing.

What is replacing them is insecurity and uncertainty. Low-paid, part-time, temporary and seasonal work; the 'feast or famine' of self-employment; the 'sharing economy', where people rent out their possessions for a pittance; the 'gig economy', where people are paid performance by performance or piece by piece. For a growing number of people, work is both low-paid and insecure, and income uncertain.[8]

The scream of outrage from America's white working/middle class that led to the election of Donald Trump is to a large extent about the disappearance of people's secure, well-paid jobs and the erosion of comfortable middle-class lifestyles. And the scream is as much from women as men. Even today, despite the advancement of women's equality, many women depend on their men for financial support, especially when the children are young. They can cope with their own income insecurity if their menfolk have steady wages. Life is very tough for families when neither women nor men have certainty of income.

Many people want to restore the secure waged jobs of the past – to resurrect manufacturing and bring back mining. But the dangerous, dirty, physically demanding jobs that were the lot of former generations are not coming back. Manufacturing no longer needs armies of drone workers on production lines, all doing the same thing day in, day out. Mining no longer needs armies of men risking their lives every day to bring scarce minerals to the surface. Robots can extract minerals and produce 'stuff' far better than humans.

All manner of policies to address the insecurity and poverty stemming from the transformation of work have been suggested. Some of them amount to modern Luddism – ban robots, maintain obsolete industries, reject new technology if it means loss of jobs. Others call for stronger trades unions and the return of collective bargaining to raise wages and improve working conditions for today's low-paid insecure workers. And some more radical ideas are gaining traction. Of these, the most prominent are wage subsidies, job guarantees and universal basic income. Criticism of these three ideas often centres on their cost and their fairness. It is beyond the scope of this book to consider their relative merits and demerits. However, for all three, QE for the People could solve the cost problem.

Job guarantees and wage subsidies financed by the central bank would act as countercyclical money supply stabilizers, since the amount of new money created would automatically increase when unemployment was high and wages low, and fall during times of rising private sector employment and wages. Universal basic income financed by the central bank would act as a different kind of stabilizer. Rather than varying with the economic cycle, the amount of money created would rise in line with inflation, thus continually increasing the money supply as suggested by Milton Friedman. It could even be automated. The income security this would provide to households would support demand and help to prevent cascading debt defaults and spending cuts in the event of a financial or economic crisis.

Would long-term helicopter money of this kind interfere with the central bank's responsibility for managing short-term demand disruption? It is hard to see why. One-off helicopter drops could still be used at need, and the central bank could still buy investment bonds or finance additional government spending. If inflation rose, the central bank could sell securities or issue bonds as well as raising interest rates. And it could still raise interest rates, tighten bank reserve and capital requirements to discourage excessive bank lending, and intervene in markets to stabilize bond yields and exchange rates. None of this would be in any way affected by long-term helicopter money given directly to people in the form of a basic income, an income subsidy or a guaranteed wage.

There is, however, a political problem. Who would set the level of a universal basic income, income subsidy or guaranteed wage? If the central bank set it without any involvement from government, the decision would lack democratic legitimacy. If the government set it, or significantly influenced it, there could be political pressure to adjust it for electoral purposes. As with all other forms of helicopter money, long-term income support schemes require cooperation between government and central bank – and that involves trust.

The fundamental weakness of any form of helicopter money is that governments can be too irresponsible to be trusted, and that central banks that don't trust government can become too detached from the real economy. This form is no exception. But that is not a reason not to use it. In demand-constrained economies where automation is bringing about fundamental change in the nature of work, permanent helicopter money may be the only way of maintaining financial stability and economic prosperity.[9]

Lessons for the Next Depression

Climate change

There is scientific consensus that the Earth's climate is warming, which is radically changing the nature of the planet.[10] There are profound implications for the future of humanity and indeed for life on earth as we know it. Already, the effects are becoming apparent: ice caps are melting, sea levels are rising, global temperatures are the highest on record and the incidence of extreme weather events is increasing. According to the Governor of the Bank of England, climate change threatens both financial stability and long-term prosperity.[11]

But greening the global economy will be phenomenally expensive, and there is very little time left in which to make a significant difference.[12] Only central banks have the power to create the quantities of money needed to decarbonize the whole world before it is too late. Central bank financing of green initiatives, low-carbon technologies and renewable energy projects undertaken by governments and public investment banks around the world may be the only realistic way of funding what will be the world's largest ever development project. If governments and central banks can conquer their fears and agree to cooperate, it may not be too late to use QE for the People to help to save the planet.

When the next crisis comes

Just as we learned from the Great Depression, so now we need to learn from the Great Experiment. We learned from the Great Depression that supporting asset prices prevents a deflationary spiral; thus was born QE for the Banks. But the Great Experiment has taught us that supporting asset prices alone does not prevent a crisis turning into long-lasting economic slump. When the next crisis comes – as it inevitably will – new money will once again have to be created to replace lost bank lending. But this time, it must go to ordinary people and productive businesses, not just into financial markets to support asset prices.

QE for the People is the most effective way of delivering monetary stimulus to a depressed economy, especially one weighed down with high levels of private and public debt. Indeed, the most frequently raised objections to QE for the People amount to fear that it might be rather too effective at bringing deflation to an end. But when the economy is falling off a cliff, or stuck in a deflationary slump, inflation should be the last thing central banks fear. Central banks' job is to deliver the necessary monetary stimulus in the most effective way available. Politicians and lawmakers need to clear away all restrictions – whether legal, ideological or cultural – that prevent central banks from doing their job.

When the next crisis hits, QE for the People – both helicopter money (or financing of the fiscal deficit) and investment bond buying – should clearly be the policy tool of choice. However, other policies have their place too, including QE for the Banks. When banks are damaged, and everyone is paying off debt and saving like crazy, both Main Street and Wall Street need new money, and central banks need to be able to use every tool at their disposal. Together, QE for the People and QE for the Banks make up 'QE for Everyone'.

Notes

1 The Great Experiment

1 Troubled Asset Relief Program (TARP) Information. https://www.federalreserve.gov/supervisionreg/tarp info.htm
2 The justification for bailing out GM and Chrysler was the potential job losses if they failed, which was estimated to be as high as one million. The Treasury eventually made a profit on the sale of Ally, but losses on GM and Chrysler. https://www.thebalance. com/auto-industry-bailout-gm-ford-chrysler-3305 670
3 'Obama alumni shed light on why so little was done to aid homeowners in crisis', Marketwatch. https:// www.marketwatch.com/story/obama-alumni-shed-li ght-on-why-so-little-was-done-to-aid-homeowners- in-crisis-2016-02-11
4 Ibid.
5 https://www.economist.com/free-exchange/2012/ 10/31/they-did-not-have-to-be-so-unfair

6 The G20's action was enormous and wide rang-
ing. http://www.imf.org/en/Publications/WP/Issues/
2018/04/11/Interest-Growth-Differentials-and-Debt-
Limits-in-Advanced-Economies-45794

The G20's measures are unfortunately seldom
credited for the fact that global growth resumed in
2010. This is despite substantial evidence that when
governments turned to austerity, growth fizzled out
and did not resume until austerity was relaxed.
Monetary economists have preferred to commend
QE and other monetary policy interventions for the
brief return of growth in 2010. They are, however,
struggling to explain why growth fizzled out and why
it took a decade of exceptionally low interest rates
and QE to restore it.

7 'The Grapes of Wrath', John Steinbeck.

8 'The Great Contraction 1929–33', Friedman and
Schwartz. https://press.princeton.edu/titles/8754.html

9 'The Great Contraction 1929–33', ibid.

10 'The Optimum Quantity of Money and Other
Essays,' Chapter 1, Milton Friedman 1969.

11 'The Optimum Quantity of Money', ibid.

12 'The Debt–Deflation Theory of Great Depressions',
Irving Fisher. https://campus.fsu.edu/bbcswebdav/
users/jcalhoun/Courses/Growth_of_American_Econ
omy/Chapter_Supplemental_Readings/Chapter_23/
Fisher-The_Debt_Deflation_Theory.pdf

13 'General Theory', John Maynard Keynes.

14 'Deflation: Making Sure "It" Doesn't Happen Here',
Bernanke. https://www.federalreserve.gov/boardDocs
/speeches/2002/20021121/default.htm

15 'Lessons from Japan: Fighting a Balance Sheet Recession', Koo 2010. https://www.cfapubs.org/doi/pdf/10.2469/cp.v27.n4.4

16 'Growth in a time of debt', Reinhart and Rogoff. http://www.nber.org/papers/w15639.pdf

17 'Does high public debt consistently stifle economic growth? A critique of Reinhart and Rogoff', Herndon, Ash and Pollin. https://www.umassmed.edu/globalassets/quantitative-health-sciences/files/camb.-j.-econ.-2013-herndon-cje-bet075.pdf

18 George Osborne, Mansion House speech 2013. https://www.gov.U.K./government/speeches/speech-by-chancellor-of-the-exchequer-rt-hon-george-osborne-mp-mansion-house-2013

19 'Verbatim of remarks made by Mario Draghi', ECB. https://www.ecb.europa.eu/press/key/date/2012/html/sp120726.en.html

20 FOMC Minutes, 16 September 2008. https://www.federalreserve.gov/monetarypolicy/fomcminutes20080916.htm

21 What 'Some Unpleasant Monetarist Arithmetic' really says is that government and central bank must cooperate. Unfortunately, the piece only considers the consequences if government and central bank don't cooperate to **reduce** inflation. It does not consider the possibility that governments might systematically undermine central bank attempts to **raise** inflation. https://www.minneapolisfed.org/research/qr/qr531.pdf

22 'When Money Dies' by Adam Fergusson is a good account of the Weimar hyperinflation.

23 For example, see 'Inflation, deflation and QE, redux', Coppola Comment. https://www.coppolacomment. com/2013/11/inflation-deflation-and-qe-redux.html

24 'The Unintended Consequences of Quantitative Easing', Jean-Michel Paul, Bloomberg. https:// www.bloomberg.com/opinion/articles/2017-08-22/ the-unintended-consequences-of-quantitative-easing Paul points out that governments have also benefited from asset price rises, so could afford to invest.

25 'US accused of forcing up world food prices', *Guardian.* https://www.theguardian.com/business/ 2010/nov/05/us-accused-of-worsening-price-rises

26 'UN to hold crisis talks on food prices as riots hit Mozambique', *Guardian.* https://www.theguardian. com/world/2010/sep/03/un-mozambique-food-prices

27 https://www.scientificamerican.com/article/climate-change-and-rising-food-prices-heightened-arab-spr ing/

28 'On the international spillovers of US Quantitative Easing,' Fratzscher, Lo Duca and Straub, Wiley. https://onlinelibrary.wiley.com/doi/pdf/10.1111/ecoj. 12435

Fratzscher et al. draw a clear distinction between QE1, during which investment flows were (slightly) **from** developing countries **to** US bonds and equities, and QE2 and QE3, during which investment flows were strongly **to** developing countries. They comment that this reflected risk-off versus risk-on behaviour, and observe that QE therefore amplifies the procyclicality of investment flows. If there were any gain for the US from this dollar drain, it would seem to be through developing country purchases of the US. Treasuries as savings vehicles for their excess dollars. This shines the spotlight on fiscal policy as the vehicle through which QE primarily achieves its effect once asset prices have been stabilized. This is consistent with macroeconomic research showing that at the zero lower bound, monetary policy is ineffective absent fiscal cooperation.

2 Understanding Money

1 This section is necessarily highly summarized. 'Just Money' by Ann Pettifor provides a deeper discussion of how money works in a modern economy.
2 'Money creation in the modern economy', McLeay, Radia and Thomas, Bank of England quarterly bulletin. https://www.bankofengland.co.uk/-/media/boe/files/quarterly-bulletin/2014/money-creation-in-the-modern-economy.pdf
3 Source: ECB Statistical Database. http://sdw.ecb.europa.eu/quickview.do;jsessionid=95AC721A8BC7A943FC94878BB4FEB28B?SERIES_KEY=124.MIR.M.U2.B.A2A.A.B.0.2240.EUR.N&start=&end=&submitOptions.x=0&submitOptions.y=0&trans=YPC
4 Source: ECB Statistical Database. http://sdw.ecb.europa.eu/home.do?chart=t1.2
5 Chart from the ECB's Statistical Database, ibid.

3 QE for the People: A Better Way

1 'Combatting Eurozone deflation: QE for the People', Muellbauer, VoXEU. https://voxeu.org/article/com batting-eurozone-deflation-qe-people
2 'Green Quantitative Easing: Paying for the Economy We Need', Richard Murphy and Colin Hines. http://www.financeforthefuture.com/GreenQuEasing.pdf
3 'Italy bank rescue marred by suicide and lost savings', BBC. https://www.bbc.com/news/world-europe-3506 2239
4 'House of Debt', Atif Mian and Amir Sufi, University of Chicago Press.
5 In practice, investors would be aware that the central bank was financing public investment projects.
6 'Bank of England to buy Apple bonds', BBC. https://www.bbc.co.U.K./news/business-37348889
7 'A Green Bank of England', Positive Money. http://positivemoney.org/wp-content/uploads/2018/05/PositiveMoney_AGreenBankofEngland_Web.pdf
8 If the securitizations were tranched, the central bank could buy the highest-rated tranches, thus protecting itself from credit risk.

4 Some (Weak) Objections to QE for the People

1 Whether the Reichsbank's money printing caused the Weimar hyperinflation is disputed. See 'Germany's 1923 Hyperinflation: a "Private" Affair', Stephen Zarlenga. https://www.wintersonnenwende.com/scriptorium/english/archives/articles/hyperinflation-e.html

2 Figures from 'The Japanese economy during the interwar period', Bank of Japan. https://www.boj.or.jp/en/research/wps_rev/rev_2009/data/rev09e02.pdf
3 Figures from 'Japanese industrial policy during the interwar period', Hideaki Miyajima. https://www.thebhc.org/sites/default/files/beh/BEHprint/v021/p0270-p0279.pdf
4 'World Hyperinflations', Hanke and Krus, Cato Institute. https://www.cato.org/publications/working-paper/world-hyperinflations
5 'Hyperinflation – It's More Than Just A Monetary Phenomenon', Cullen Roche. https://papers.ssrn.com/sol3/papers.cfm?abstract_id=1799102
6 Interview with Otmar Issing in 'Helikoptergeld wäre Bankrotterklärung', Frankfurter Allgemeine. https://www.faz.net/aktuell/wirtschaft/ex-ezb-chef-volkswirt-otmar-issing-warnt-vor-helikoptergeld-14141309.html
7 Quoted in 'The Life and Times of Korekiyo Takahashi', *Wall Street Journal*. https://blogs.wsj.com/japanrealtime/2015/06/11/wsj-archive-the-life-and-times-of-korekiyo-takahashi/
8 'Conventional' QE requires monetary and fiscal authorities to cooperate too, to ensure that there are sufficient government bonds of the right tenor for the central bank to buy. One of the biggest problems the ECB has encountered in its QE programme is the lack of cooperation from some governments, which has caused critical shortages of some types of bonds.
9 'Debt and the Devil', Adair Turner.
10 Oral evidence to the Economic Affairs Committee of

the House of Lords, Dr Mark Carney, April 2016. http://data.parliament.U.K./writtenevidence/committ eeevidence.svc/evidencedocument/economic-affairs-co mmittee/governor-of-the-bank-of-england-2016/oral/ 32343.pdf

11 'Different types of central bank insolvency and the central role of seigniorage', Reis. http://www.nber. org/papers/w21226.pdf

12 As discussed in Reis, ibid.

13 'Koo on why helicopter money just won't work', FT Alphaville. https://ftalphaville.ft.com/2016/07/27/21 70980/koo-on-why-helicopter-money-just-wont-work/

14 'How much did the 2009 Australian Fiscal Stimulus Boost Demand?', Leigh. http://andrewleigh.org/pdf/ fiscalstimulus.pdf

The survey covers both the 2008 cash drop and a larger stimulus package of tax cuts and benefit increases in 2009. As the results are similar for both, I have treated both as helicopter money for the purposes of this piece, although as neither was central bank financed any increase in the money supply could have come only from increased bank lending. A significant proportion of Australians paid off debt, but this was offset by a corresponding rise in government debt. In effect, because the central bank was not involved, Australian household debts were transferred to the government.

15 'The Simple Analytics of Helicopter Money: Why it Works – Always', Willem Buiter. http://www. economics-ejournal.org/economics/discussionpapers/ 2014-24/file

16 Since the 'redemption' would constitute settlement of a claim, the Bank of England would give legal tender. Bank of England notes are legal tender in England and Wales, but not in Scotland. However, coins are legal tender everywhere in the UK. Thus, the Bank might give coins rather than notes in settlement.

17 'Credibility and Monetary Policy in a Liquidity Trap (Wonkish)', Paul Krugman. https://krugman.blogs. nytimes.com/2011/03/18/credibility-and-monetary-policy-in-a-liquidity-trap-wonkish/

18 Eric Lonergan has made this argument powerfully. See 'Legal helicopter drops in the Eurozone', Philosophy of Money. https://www.philosophyof money.net/legal-helicopter-drops-in-the-eurozone/

19 Article 123 of the Lisbon Treaty prohibits all forms of central bank financing of government spending. http://www.lisbon-treaty.org/wcm/the-lisbon-treaty/ treaty-on-the-functioning-of-the-european-union-and -comments/part-3-union-policies-and-internal-action s/title-viii-economic-and-monetary-policy/chapter-1-economic-policy/391-article-123.html

20 'The UK's Productivity Problem: Hub No Spokes', Andrew Haldane. https://www.bankofengland.co.uk/ -/media/boe/files/speech/2018/the-uks-productivity-problem-hub-no-spokes-speech-by-andy-haldane

21 'The Economic Scars of Crises and Recessions', IMF. https://blogs.imf.org/2018/03/21/the-economic-scars-of-crises-and-recessions/

22 'GDP-linked bonds and sovereign default', Barr, Bush and Pienkowski, Bank of England. https://

www.bankofengland.co.uk/-/media/boe/files/work
ing-paper/2014/gdp-linked-bonds-and-sovereign-
default.pdf?la=en&hash=E44CC8AAAD2B629DB1
233DAF3A83330611C32325

23 'Interest-Growth Differentials and Debt Limits in Advanced Countries', Barratt, IMF. http://www.imf. org/en/Publications/WP/Issues/2018/04/11/Interest-Growth-Differentials-and-Debt-Limits-in-Advanced-Economies-45794

24 'The Household Fallacy', Farmer and Zabczyk, NIESR. https://www.niesr.ac.U.K./sites/default/files/ publications/DP487_0.pdf

25 'Technical Features of Outright Monetary Trans actions', ECB. https://www.ecb.europa.eu/press/pr/ date/2012/html/pr120906_1.en.html

26 'The Goldman Touch,' Coppola Comment. http:// www.coppolacomment.com/2014/12/the-goldman-touch.html

27 Automatic stabilizers are typically welfare payments such as unemployment benefit that automatically rise during economic downturns and fall during economic booms. They are an essential part of coun-tercyclical fiscal policy.

5 Lessons for the Next Depression

1 'A *Monetary* and *Fiscal* Framework for Economic Stability', Friedman, 1948.

2 'Pensions at a Glance', 2017 edition, OECD. https:// www.oecd-ilibrary.org/docserver/pension_glance-20 17-en.pdf?expires=1531483231&id=id&accname=g

uest&checksum=F88D91B653BFBDF3143A76243C
393632

3 See, for example, Jared Dillian, 'Japan has entered the next phase: Unlimited money printing', *Forbes* magazine. https://www.forbes.com/sites/jareddillian/2017/07/10/japan-has-entered-the-next-phase-unlimited-money-printing/#598e667d68a0

4 See Adair Turner, 'Rethinking the Monetization Taboo'. https://www.socialeurope.eu/monetization

5 In his book 'Debt and the Devil', Turner calls debt monetization/deficit financing 'Overt Monetary Finance'.

6 Much of this section comes from a piece about Japan that I wrote in November 2013 for the (now defunct) online magazine *Pieria*. The piece was called 'The Land of the Setting Sun', hence the references to sunset.

7 'The Hourglass and the Escalator', AFGAS/Work Foundation, 2011.

8 As discussed by, for example, Guy Standing in 'The Precariat'.

9 'The Changing Nature of Work', Coppola Comment. https://www.coppolacomment.com/2012/08/the-changing-nature-of-work.html

10 'Scientific Consensus: Earth's Climate Is Warming', NASA. https://climate.nasa.gov/scientific-consensus/

11 'Breaking the Tragedy of the Horizon', Mark Carney, 2015. https://www.bankofengland.co.U.K./-/media/boe/files/speech/2015/breaking-the-tragedy-of-the-horizon-climate-change-and-financial-stability.pdf?la=en&hash=7C67E785651862457D99511147C7424FF5EA0C1A

12 'We have 12 years to limit climate change catastro-phe, warns UN', *Guardian*. https://www.theguardian.com/environment/2018/oct/08/global-warming-must-not-exceed-15c-warns-landmark-un-report